THE

© Wyatt North Publishing, LLC 2019

Publishing by Wyatt North Publishing, LLC. A Boutique Publishing Company.

"Wyatt North" and "A Boutique Publishing Company" are trademarks of Wyatt North Publishing, LLC.

Copyright © Wyatt North Publishing, LLC. All rights reserved, including the right to reproduce this book or portions thereof in any form whatsoever. For more information please visit http://www.WyattNorth.com.

Cover design by Wyatt North Publishing, LLC. Copyright © Wyatt North Publishing, LLC. All rights reserved.

Scripture texts in this work are taken from the *New American Bible, revised edition*© 2010, 1991, 1986, 1970 Confraternity of Christian Doctrine, Washington, D.C. and are used by permission of the copyright owner. All Rights Reserved. No part of the New American Bible may be reproduced in any form without permission in writing

Introduction: The Archangels 4

Chapter 1: A Truth of Faith...7

Chapter 2: Saint Michael – "Who Can Compare to God?" ...19

Chapter 3: Saint Gabriel – "God Is My Strength" 31

Chapter 4: Saint Raphael – "God Heals" 43

Chapter 5: Apocryphal Archangels...55

Chapter 6: Angelic Devotion and Prayer....................................83

Chapter 7: Picturing Archangels..102

Conclusion: Messages from the Archangels 118

Introduction:
The Archangels

A recent Gallup poll revealed that 72% of American adults believe in angels. Angels are everywhere—there are numerous popular television shows and movies about them. During the Christmas season, many of us watch *It's a Wonderful Life*, rooting for Clarence the angel to earn his wings. Angels grace the covers of a wide range of books, ranging from volumes offering information about their names to fantastic stories employing them as characters. While these stories vary from heartwarming to dark, the angels tend to be depicted in a consistent fashion: with human features, broad wings, and occasionally, a halo.

But where did the information reflected in these books and images originate? While many representations of angels are connected to enjoyable entertainment, much of it is just Hollywood fiction, not reality. As Catholics, we do not need to rely on Hollywood for information about the Archangels, as we can consult Sacred Scripture, tradition, and Church teachings to learn the truth about these powerful beings.

We will explore scriptural references to the Archangels to study the divine messages they bring. We will discover Church teachings that guide us in our interactions with angels and, as a consequence, deepen our relationship with God. Moreover, we will look at how angels can intercede in our lives and how we can speak to them through prayer. We will consider a variety of devotional practices, such as contemplating sacred art or praying chaplets.

Angels are, indeed, everywhere. Their purpose is to serve God and guide us. They are formidable warriors against evil, guardians of the whole of God's creation, witnesses to God's sacred mysteries, and messengers of God's salvation.

Chapter 1:
A Truth of Faith

Angels are real. The Catechism of the Catholic Church states, "The existence of the spiritual, non-corporeal beings that Sacred Scripture usually calls 'angels' is a truth of faith. The witness of Scripture is as clear as the unanimity of Tradition." In other words, to be Catholic is to believe in the reality of angels.

Pope John Paul II, quoting a modern theologian, observed that "if one wishes to get rid of the angels, one must radically revise Sacred Scripture itself, and with it the whole history of salvation." Angels appear throughout the Old and New Testaments. The Catechism says that angels surround Christ and serve him in the "accomplishment of his saving mission to man." Christ is "the center of the angelic world," and angels belong to him because "he made them messengers of his saving plan."

Spiritual Creatures

God made two orders of creatures from nothing: "the spiritual and the corporeal, the angelic and the earthly." We affirm this reality every time we attend Mass and recite the Nicene-Constantinopolitan Creed: "I believe in one God, the Father Almighty, Creator of heaven and earth, of all that is seen and unseen." As the Catechism of the Catholic Church explains: "The angels are purely spiritual creatures, incorporeal, invisible, immortal, and personal beings endowed with intelligence and will. They ceaselessly contemplate God face-to-face and they glorify him."

The Catechism says that the "human creature" is a hybrid being, "composed of spirit and body." Pope John Paul II, in his catechesis on angels, said that humans belong to the visible world due to our bodies, but our "spiritual soul which vivifies the body" places us "on the boundary between the visible and invisible creation." He goes on to explain that angels are purely spiritual and "therefore not proper to the visible world even though present and working therein. They constitute a world apart." Because angels are pure spirit, with no physical body, they are neither male nor female. Many theologians, or "angelogians," have discussed whether each individual angel could be considered a species in itself. Saint Thomas Aquinas espoused this view, stating that one angel differs from another angel the way a daisy differs from a tulip; they are unique.

Human beings, no matter how virtuous, do not turn into angels when they die. Angels and humans are completely different species and cannot morph into one another. When a human's body dies, his or her soul, being immortal, lives on with God; that soul does not turn into an angel. It is easy to confuse our human soul with an angel, as neither is physical—both are unseen. Neither can ever die; neither has weight or any other physical attribute. A soul that goes to heaven lives with God, the angels, and other human souls. A human can become a saint, but not an angel, when he or she dies. Pope John Paul II noted that through encounters with the world of angels, humans come to see their own beings not only as body, but also as spirit.

God's Messengers

The word "angel" comes from the Latin *angelus* and the Greek *angelos*, both of which are translations of the Hebrew *mal'akh*, which means "one sent," "messenger," or "ambassador." The term "angel" is more descriptive of what they *do*, because what they *are* is pure spirit. Saint Augustine observed that "angel" is the name of their office, not of their nature. The Catechism says "with their whole beings the angels are servants and messengers of God." Throughout the Bible, angels deliver God's message of love and salvation to us.

The purpose of every angel is to serve, praise, worship, and pray to God. In the course of serving God, through God's grace, they also pray for us, support us, protect us, and offer us guidance. Angels are not to be worshipped in themselves; we worship only God. Consider the passages in Revelation where an angel appears and John bows to worship him. In each instance, the angel says, "Don't do that! I am a fellow servant with you and with your brothers and sisters who hold to the testimony of Jesus. Worship God! For it is the Spirit of prophecy who bears testimony to Jesus" (Revelation 19:10) and "Don't do that! I am a fellow servant with you and with your fellow prophets and with all who keep the words of this scroll. Worship God!" (Revelation 22:8).

Nine Choirs

A hierarchy of angels exists, and this hierarchy is divided into nine sections or choirs. Above the choirs of angels, as above all other created beings, is the Virgin Mary, also known as Our Lady of the Angel. Pope John Paul II teaches that angels are "divided into orders and grades," which correspond to the "measure of their perfection and to the tasks entrusted to them." He further points out that theologians do not "attribute an absolute value to them" and there may be elements we cannot know, given that we are limited by our senses when trying to understand spirit, which cannot be grasped with the senses. This hierarchy is not official dogma, but comes to us through tradition and the work of many Church scholars from Saint Dionysius the Areopagite to Saint Thomas Aquinas. It is a traditional and accepted Catholic belief.

The first sphere, focused on the praise and worship of God, includes Seraphim, Cherubim, and Thrones. Seraphim are the highest choir, and they understand God with the deepest comprehension. Their name means "the burning or fiery ones," so hot does their love for God burn. Cherubim are described in Ezekiel 1:5–11 as creatures with six wings.

They also contemplate God, but focus on God's providence and his divine plan for Creation. Their name means "fullness of wisdom." Thrones are also known as "ophanim," which in Hebrew means "those of the wheel." Daniel 7:9 describes them as a fiery wheel within a wheel, the rims of which are covered with hundreds of eyes. Thrones contemplate God's power and justice.

The second sphere's choirs work to bring to fruition God's plans for the universe. Dominions (or Dominations) govern the angels that serve as intermediaries between God and other creatures. Their name means "authority," and they also preside over nations and places. The Dominions govern the Virtues, whose name means "power, might or energy." Saint Thomas Aquinas describes this choir of angelic beings as governing every natural force, cycle, and motion; in other words, they manage and support the order of the universe. Powers, also known as "Authorities," are warriors who defend humanity from evil spirits.

The final three choirs focus on interacting directly with human beings. Principalities take care of particular groups, such as countries, cities, or ethnicities. They serve as guardian angels for these groups or associated regions, influencing leaders and cultures. Archangels are the least-well-defined group in this sphere. They tend to be guardians for special people or carry messages of utmost importance. The last choir in this sphere comprises the Angels, which are the closest to the material earth and to human beings. These are the guardian angels, one of whom is assigned to each human being. They act on our behalf by praying for us to God, and they help deliver God's responses to our prayers. They seek to assist those who ask for help and are the most involved with human beings on a regular basis.

The nine choirs together form the "hosts of heaven," or God's army. God is called "Lord of Hosts," or *Yahweh Sabaoth* in Hebrew, more than three hundred times in the Old Testament and twice in the New Testament (see Romans 9:29 and James 5:4).

Seven Archangels

In the Book of Tobit, Saint Raphael reveals that seven angels stand before God (Tobit 12:15). In Revelation 8:2, these seven angels are mentioned again: "And I saw the seven angels who stand before God, and seven trumpets were given to them." According to Church tradition and teaching, these are references to the seven Archangels.

There is no agreement on exactly how these seven Archangels fit in with the "choir" of Archangels. Some say the seven to which Scripture refers are part of the choir of Archangels. Other scholars say the term "archangel" is a translation of the Hebrew *ray-mal'akh*, which means "chief angel," and interpret that to mean they lead the angelic host. The designation "Archangel" in this instance indicates their leadership role, rather than their choir. Some argue that these powerful angels are from the choir of Seraphim. Again, there is no agreement, and this detail is not explained in Scripture. It is one of the many things about the Archangels we cannot know for certain.

The Church does acknowledge that there are seven Archangels, as evidenced by Scripture and practice. However, only three are named in Scripture: Raphael, Michael, and Gabriel. A fourth Archangel, Uriel, is named in the Book of Enoch, apocalyptic literature that is outside the biblical canon. Uriel was well-known by many Church Fathers and venerated in the early Catholic Church.

The remaining three are listed with a wide variety of names, depending on the tradition consulted. While there is one list of seven that the Church lent a certain amount of recognition (in 1720, a church in Bavaria received canonical permission to dedicate seven altars to the Archangels), the Church discourages naming any angel beyond the three names we are given in Scripture. Devotion to the Archangels named in the Bible—Michael, Raphael, and Gabriel—is encouraged.

Naming Angels

Recently, the popularity of various forms of New Age thought revived these additional angelic names. In response, the Vatican issued a 330-page Directory of Public Piety in 2002. It said, "The practice of assigning names to the Holy Angels should be discouraged, except in the cases of Gabriel, Raphael and Michael whose names are contained in Holy Scripture." Banning the veneration of angels that do not appear in Scripture seeks to defuse the influence that New Age thought and angel worship might cause.

For instance, some New Age thought encourages naming our guardian angels to become more "familiar" with them. The Directory found this to be a distraction from the real purpose of venerating angels, which is to deepen our relationship with God. It said "the practice of giving particular names to angels, with the exception of Michael, Gabriel and Raphael, is to be disapproved of. Popular piety towards angels, which is legitimate and healthy, can nevertheless sometimes lead to deviations."

These "deviations" are basically distractions from the practices that cultivate a healthy spiritual life. They can lead to feeling "at the mercy of superior forces" of angels and demons and feeling helpless. In fact, these views bear little relation to the true Gospel vision of the struggle to overcome the devil, "which requires moral commitment, a fundamental option for the Gospel, humility and prayer."

They can also discourage us from "our progressive maturing on the journey toward Christ" if we "simplistically" or "childishly" ascribe all setbacks to the devil and all success to the guardian angels.

This is not a new concern for the Vatican. In AD 745, Pope Saint Zachary led a local council (or synod) in Rome in which he sought to curb a growing tendency toward angel worship; many angels were venerated by name at the time. The council declared that divine authority acknowledges only three angel names: Michael, Gabriel, and Raphael. The Roman Church rejected the Fourth Esdras, which frequently mentions Uriel; therefore, the name Uriel was rejected. Later, in AD 789, the Council of Aix-la-Chapelle also forbade the naming of angels outside the three mentioned in Scripture.

A "Cult" of Angels

Pope John Paul II notes that "the Church honors the figures of three angels with a liturgical cult; these are called by name in Sacred Scripture." While the term "cult" has taken on unpleasant and derogatory connotations of late, that is not the way the Pope uses the term here. The term "cult" derives from the Latin word *cultus*, which literally means "care." Accordingly, the main meaning of the term "cult" refers to the care, relationship, and devotion owed to holy beings that is expressed through various prayers, actions, or rites. In this context, it is not about "brain-washing," but about a thoughtful and contemplative way to venerate saints (including angels).

Michael, Gabriel, and Raphael are all recognized as "saints." While they were never formally canonized, they are angelic persons and holy by their nature. The word "saint" comes from the Latin word *sancta*, which means "holy." While all the heavenly angels are holy, we only know the names of these three, so they are honored with the title of Saint.

The names of the Archangels all end in "-el," which means "of God." Their names tend to describe the focus of what they do or the type of messenger work they perform. Pope John Paul II summarizes them as follows:

"The first is *Michael the Archangel* (cf. Daniel 10:13–20; Revelation 12:7; Jude 9). His name is a synthesis that expresses the essential attitude of the good spirits. "Mica-EL" in fact means: "Who is like God?" In this name, therefore, we find expressed the salvific choice thanks to which the angels "see the face of the Father" who is in heaven.

The second is *Gabriel*, a figure bound specially to the mystery of the Incarnation of the Son of God (cf. Luke 1:19–26). His name means "my power is God" or "power of God," as if to say that the culmination of creation, the Incarnation, is the supreme sign of the omnipotent Father.

Finally, the third archangel is called *Raphael.* "Rafa-EL" means "God heals." He is made known to us by the story of Tobias in the Old Testament (cf. Tobit 12:15–20) which is significant for what it says about entrusting to the angels the little children of God, who are always in need of custody, care, and protection.

If we reflect well, we see that each one of these figures—Mica-EL, Gabri-EL, and Rafa-EL—reflects in a particular way the truth contained in the question posed by the author of the Letter to the Hebrews: "Are they not all ministering spirits sent forth to serve, for the sake of those who are to possess salvation?" (Hebrews 1–14).

Chapter 2:
Saint Michael –
"Who Can Compare to God?"

The Archangel Michael is probably the best-known of the Archangels. He appears in Scripture in Revelation, the Book of Daniel, and the Epistle of Saint Jude. He is also mentioned in numerous Jewish and Christian apocalyptic sources.

Based on the descriptions in Scripture, Christian tradition has assigned four offices to Saint Michael: 1) to fight against Satan, 2) to rescue souls from the devil, especially at the hour of death, 3) to be the guardian angel of the Church and champion of God's people, and 4) to weigh souls on Judgment Day.

War in Heaven

Revelation 12:7 begins with a powerful narrative description: "Then war broke out in heaven; Michael and his angels battled against the dragon." Chapter 12 in Revelation continues the story of the fallen angels. The dragon and its angels did not prevail, and "there was no longer any place for them in heaven. The huge dragon, the ancient serpent, who is called the Devil and Satan, who deceived the whole world, was thrown down to earth, and its angels were thrown down with it" (Revelation 12:7–9). The Hebrew word *satan* means "to obstruct," "to oppose," or "act as an adversary," and it became the name of the leader of the fallen angels who challenged God.

Satan's sin was pride. He did not want to love and serve God; he wanted to be as great as God. In Milton's seventeenth-century epic poem *Paradise Lost*, the devil declares, "I will not serve!" (*Non serviam!* in Latin). The battle cry against Satan's boastful claim was "*Michael*," which in Hebrew means "Who is like God?" The answer to the question, of course, is nobody—God is Supreme. Michael's name can also be translated as "Who can compare to God?" or "Who is like God?" As the Prince of the Angels, he is often depicted with a shield that bears his name in Latin: *Quis ut Deus*.

God did not create Satan to be evil. When God created angels and humans, he gave us free will. Pope John Paul II says that the love both angels and humans have for God is an act of free will. Love for God "is an act of a free will, and therefore for the angels also freedom implies a possibility of choice for or against the Good, which they know, that is, God himself." He goes on to say that "by creating free beings, God willed that there should be realized in the world *true love* which is possible *only on the basis of freedom*." Because both humans and angels have the ability to choose love or not, we have the capacity to sin. Tradition tells us the angels made their choices either to serve God or to reject Him when they were created.

Pope Benedict XVI elaborates on Michael's role in Revelation: "He defends the cause of God's oneness against the presumption of the dragon, the 'ancient serpent', as John calls it. The serpent's continuous effort is to make men believe that God must disappear so that they themselves may become important; that God impedes our freedom and, therefore, that we must rid ourselves of him." Michael's battle reminds us that we too may find ourselves wrapped up in ego, thinking we are too busy or stressed in our earthly lives to make time for prayer and service to God.

Pope Benedict XVI further points out that "the dragon does not only accuse God. The Book of Revelation also calls it 'the accuser of our brothers…, who accuses them before our God day and night' (Revelation 12:10). Those who cast God aside do not make man great but divest him of his dignity. Man then becomes a failed product of evolution. Those who accuse God also accuse man. Faith in God defends man in all his frailty and short-comings: God's brightness shines on every individual… And what more could one say and think about man than the fact that God himself was made man?" Without God, we cannot be great or achieve the potential God invested within us. This is the same mistake Satan made—in rejecting God, insisting on the delusion he could go it alone, he became nothing.

Battle on Earth

Saint Michael did not stop battling the devil once he was cast out of heaven. Revelation 12:12 says, "But woe to you, earth and sea, for the Devil has come down to you in great fury, for he knows he has but a short time." Michael defeated Satan when he ejected him from heaven, and he will also win the final battle with Satan at the end of times.

Tradition holds that the archangel Michael appears again later in Revelation, though he is not mentioned by name. He is often identified as the angel from Revelation 20:1–3, who comes down from heaven holding "the key to the abyss and a heavy chain." The angel seizes "the dragon, the ancient serpent, which is the Devil or Satan," ties it up, and locks it in the abyss "so that it could no longer lead the nations astray." Until Michael wins this final battle at the time of the Second Coming, God has commanded him to continue the war against Satan on earth.

Guardian Angel of the Church

In times of challenge and crisis for the Church, the world, and all the faithful, devotion to Saint Michael, the Guardian Angel of the Church, is essential. Under the Old Covenant, Michael was the Guardian of the chosen people, the Jews; under the New Covenant, he performs the same function for the Church and all her members. It is in this role that he is invoked by and for the dying, as he protects the soul from the devil. Michael helps support us in our faith and guides us to humbly choose God. We, too, are called to support and pray not just for individuals, but also for the Church and all of the institutions and creatures in our universe.

Early Church Fathers often spoke to the importance of Archangels in protecting institutions and nations. For instance, Theodoret of Cyr (393–466) said in his *Interpretation of Daniel*, "We are taught that each one of us is entrusted to the care of an individual angel to guard and protect us, and to deliver us from the snares of evil demons. Archangels are entrusted with the tasks of guarding nations, as the Blessed Moses taught, and with those remarks the Blessed Daniel is in accord; for he himself speaks of 'the chief of the Kingdom of the Persians,' and a little later of 'the chief of the Greeks,' while he calls Michael the chief of Israel."

Book of Daniel

Daniel is a pious Jew who suffers persecution. The Book of Daniel describes how the faithful will be saved and encourages them to endure even during difficult times. While set during the Babylonian Exile of the sixth century B.C., the book was actually written during a similar crisis, when Antiochus IV Epiphanes (reign 175–164 B.C.), was persecuting Jews. Antiochus IV wanted to Hellenize the Jews of Palestine by forcing them to convert to the pagan religion of the realm. This conflict between the Jews and paganism is the background of the Book of Daniel. The message in all twelve chapters is that God does not abandon those who believe in Him.

Michael is referred to as "one of the chief princes" three times in the Old Testament: in Daniel 10:13, 10:21, and 12:1. Here the term "prince" refers to angelic guardians of kingdoms or places. We see that Michael is the patron angel and protector of Israel.

It is the Archangel Gabriel who first names Michael, telling Daniel in a vision that "the prince of the kingdom of Persia stood in my way for twenty-one days, until finally Michael, one of the chief princes, came to help me" (Daniel 10:13). The prince of the kingdom of Persia is the angelic guardian of Persia. Whereas some ancient texts speak of the gods of various countries (such as Deuteronomy 32:8), Daniel here refers to these spirits as "princes." Gabriel was in conflict with the "prince of the kingdom of Persia," and Michael came to his aid so he, Gabriel, could appear to Daniel.

Gabriel continues, telling Daniel "when I leave, the prince of Greece will come; but I shall tell you what is written in the book of truth. No one supports me against these except Michael, your prince..." (Daniel 10:21). Gabriel refers to Michael as "your prince," as Daniel is from Israel, the country Michael protects. Gabriel came to Daniel to give him the vision so he could see what would happen to the Jews in "the last days."

Michael's last mention in Daniel refers to the Resurrection of Jesus Christ: "at that time there shall arise Michael, the great prince, guardian of your people..." (Daniel 12:1). These passages describe Michael as the guardian angel of Israel and indicate that Michael fights against the spiritual forces that act against and threaten Israel. This scriptural occurrence also refers to the traditional understanding of Michael's presence during the judgment of souls after death.

Humility

The next place in Scripture where we see Michael is the Epistle of Saint Jude, also called the Letter of the Apostle Saint Jude Thaddeus. This is a very short letter, with an urgent message warning against false teachers. Instead of listening to God's Word, such teachers seek to interpret piety and service in their own way. These false teachers deny Christ through their pride and lead to a variety of sinful behavior. He criticizes the pseudo-teachers and says they will be punished for their sins, like the wicked angels who were cast from heaven.

Jude continues: "Similarly, these dreamers nevertheless also defile the flesh, scorn lordship, and revile glorious beings. Yet the archangel Michael, when he argued with the devil in a dispute over the body of Moses, did not venture to pronounce a reviling judgment upon him but said, 'May the Lord rebuke you!'" (Jude 8–9). Michael's modesty and willingness to be led by God stand in stark contrast to the pride of these "teachers" who would judge others according to their own standards.

In this passage, Saint Jude is referring to an apocryphal story about the Assumption of Moses. Scripture tells us Moses "was buried in a valley in the land of Moab, opposite Beth-peor; to this day no one knows the place of his burial" (Deuteronomy 34:6). The apocryphal account adds that the Archangel Michael was sent by God to bury Moses. Satan challenged the burial because he declared authority over all physical matter, which would include the body of Moses. Michael responded, "May Adonai rebuke you, for it was God's Spirit which created the world and all mankind." Satan also said that Moses was a murderer since he killed the Egyptian overseer, meaning Moses did not deserve a proper burial.

Michael gave the entire situation up to God. As he interacted with the devil, he did not accuse or slander him. Michael could have criticized his opponent, whose motives were poor, but Michael instead treated him with respect. He did not speak in derogatory terms, unlike the prideful false teachers (Jude 9). Rather, he left it to God to rebuke the devil, as God created the universe and it is his to judge. Michael is humble regarding his role in service to God.

God had Michael bury Moses so nobody could find his body, not even Satan. We see from Saint Jude's admonition that God did not want people to turn the grave site into a shrine or worship Moses' body. Satan sought to tempt the Jewish people into hero-worship by disclosing the burial site. In dealing with the devil and evil, we seek to emulate Michael and give ourselves not to anger or name-calling, but to God.

The *Assumption of Moses* is part of the Pseudepigrapha, a collection of stories that were once believed to be written by biblical people like Enoch, Noah, or Moses. It tells the story of Deuteronomy 31–34. The only extant copy was discovered in 1861 and is a Latin translation of the Greek. It is incomplete and illegible in places. The early Church Fathers would have been familiar with the book, and the Pseudepigrapha was quoted often during the time Saint Jude was writing.

Angelic Rank

Michael is the only angel in the Bible explicitly described as an Archangel (in Jude 9). In terms of his rank in the celestial hierarchy, there are many differing opinions. Saint Basil (fourth century) and other Greek Fathers set Michael at the top of the hierarchy, above all other angels. They say he is the only one in Scripture referred to as an Archangel because he is the Prince of the Heavenly Hosts, the Army of God. Pope Leo XIII's Prayer to Saint Michael echoes this sentiment. That is, Michael is considered the leader or commander of all the angels in heaven.

Others, such as Saint Bonaventura in the thirteenth century, believe he is the prince of the Seraphim, the first of the nine angelic orders. However, Saint Thomas Aquinas says he is the prince of the last and lowest choir, the angels. Some argue that he is called an Archangel out of respect and it is not indicative of his actual rank. Other traditions say he was the first angel created, which is why he is often revered as the eldest or leader of the other Archangels.

When considering all these varying opinions on Michael's angelic rank, it is helpful to keep in mind the advice that Saint Thomas Aquinas offers in the *Summa Theologiae*. He tells us that our knowledge and understanding of angels is imperfect and a complete understanding of their hierarchy and duties is not always accessible to us. This acknowledgment allows us to let go of grasping for a particular answer and focus on what is truly important: that Saint Michael fights to protect the Church and our souls from evil through the direction and love of God. Regardless of his actual rank, Michael has always been considered the greatest of all the angels in both Christian and Jewish sources.

Patron Saint

Michael is considered a Holy General and, as such, is the patron saint of soldiers, police officers, and firefighters. He is often named as a special patron in military battles. For example, when Saint Joan of Arc (1412–1431 A.D.) led French military forces in the Hundred Years' War, she received many visions from a number of saints. She said that Michael's apparitions helped her learn military strategy.

The Archangel Michael is also the patron and protector of many geographical locations, such as Cornwall, England. A tremendous variety of professions and activities also look to Michael as their patron. These vary wildly from hat makers to bankers.

He is sometimes invoked as the patron saint of cemeteries, due to his reputation as one of the angels present at the time of death, his role in protecting human souls from the devil, and his task of accompanying souls to judgment.

In his warrior capacity, he is invoked for assistance or protection against temptations, the powers of evil, and storms at sea.

Chapter 3:
Saint Gabriel –
"God Is My Strength"

Gabriel is the messenger who brings the good news of salvation. He is the angel who appears to Mary, Zachariah, and Joseph to announce the Incarnation of Christ.

This Archangel's name comes from the Hebrew verb *gabar*, which means "to be strong and mighty" or "to prevail." It is often used to describe a mighty or valiant man or hero. Thus, we might also translate Gabriel's name to mean "Might of God," "Strength of God," "My power is God," or "My hero is God." His Latin name, *Fortitudo Dei*, means "Strength of God" or "God's strength."

Pope Francis points out that the strength Gabriel offers is the spirit of knowledge: "his focus is to reveal the knowledge of God's Truth to the world. Gabriel teaches us and reminds us of God's Plan." He is a messenger of earth-shaking, monumental news. It takes strength to bear this news, and Gabriel demonstrates that in his support of the Holy Family. Gabriel helps us on our journey, especially when we feel overwhelmed by "so much bad news or news with no substance." We forget the Good News, that of the Gospel. Gabriel reminds us that Jesus came to save us, and that reminder gives us strength.

Book of Daniel

We first meet Gabriel in the Old Testament, the history of God's chosen people. In Daniel 8:15–17, the Archangel arrives to assist Daniel in understanding a vision about a

Ram and He-goat that addresses the future of the Persian and Greek empires. Daniel says that "one who looked like a man stood before me" and then a voice cries out, "Gabriel, explain the vision to this man." The word "man" in this passage has also been translated as "manlike figure." The angel's presence and majesty is so great that Daniel falls to the ground in awe. Daniel, as a pious Jew struggling with persecution due to his faith, continues to love and praise God in spite of the hardships he experiences, and he prays for God's grace and guidance.

Later, Gabriel returns while Daniel is praying and gives him the "seventy weeks of years" prophecy regarding Israel's future (Daniel 9:21-27). Though Gabriel is again identified as a "man," he is described in a way that is angelic: "Gabriel, whom I had seen in vision before, came to me in flight." Gabriel tells Daniel, "I have now come to give you understanding." However, Gabriel makes sure to emphasize that the knowledge he brings comes not from him, but from God: "An answer was given which I have come to announce, because you are beloved." In other words, the answer is coming from God; Gabriel is only the messenger.

This message is in response to Daniel's prayer, where he acknowledges the sins of Israel against God and asks for God's mercy. The "understanding" Gabriel brings is a vision regarding Israel's future—the pending future salvation of the long-awaited Messiah. God does not abandon those to trust in Him, though the path to salvation may be long and difficult. Gabriel is the messenger of the coming of the

Messiah, Jesus Christ, and offers succor and support during difficult times. We are able to emulate Saint Gabriel by consoling those who suffer, especially when they suffer due to their faith.

The Annunciation

Gabriel appeared to Daniel and prophesied the coming of the Messiah and the destruction of Jerusalem. However, as important as he is in the Old Testament, Gabriel is best-known for his role in the conception and birth of Jesus Christ. It was the Archangel Gabriel who appeared to the Virgin Mary and told her she would be the mother of the Son of God.

We meet Gabriel again in the New Testament in Luke. Here, his message from the Book of Daniel comes to fruition in the Gospel of Luke 1:11–38.

First, Gabriel appears to Zachary (or Zechariah) while the latter is praying in the Temple of Jerusalem—an "angel of the Lord appeared to him." Seeing Gabriel, he "was startled and was gripped with fear." But Gabriel tells him not to be afraid and that his "prayer has been heard. Your wife Elizabeth will bear you a son, and you are to call him John." The name "John" means "Yahweh has shown favor," indicating John's role in our salvation. Gabriel says the child will "make ready a people prepared for the Lord." In other words, John will lead the way for the Messiah, Jesus Christ.

Zechariah questions Gabriel, as his wife, Elizabeth, is "well along in years." The angel replies, "I am Gabriel. I stand in the presence of God, and I have been sent to speak to you and to tell you this good news." Elizabeth then conceives John the Baptist.

In the sixth month of Elizabeth's pregnancy, "God sent the angel Gabriel to Nazareth, a town in Galilee." The angel appears to the Virgin Mary and says, "Greetings, you who are highly favored! The Lord is with you." Gabriel tells Mary that she will conceive a son who "will be called Son of the Most High" and "of his kingdom there will be no end." Mary is told to name her child Jesus, or *Yeshua* in Hebrew, which means "Yahweh is salvation."

Mary asks how this will be possible, since she is a virgin. Gabriel tells her the Holy Spirit will come to her and her child will be holy, "the Son of God." "I am the Lord's servant," Mary answers. "May your word to me be fulfilled." Mary thus gives her *fiat*, or consent; she has a choice, and she chooses to love and serve God, regardless of how difficult the path might be. She says "yes" to God.

Gabriel tells Mary of Elizabeth's pregnancy with John the Baptist to convince her that "nothing will be impossible for

God." He assures both Zechariah and Mary that the messages he has to deliver are God's Word, not his own: "For no word from God will ever fail" (Luke 1:37).

Some Fathers of the Church believe it was Saint Gabriel who invited the shepherds of Bethlehem to adore the newborn Jesus. In Luke 2:9–14, an angel arrives to tell the shepherds about the birth of Jesus. Then, "suddenly there was a multitude of the heavenly host with the angel, praising God and saying 'Glory to God in the highest, and on earth peace to those on whom his favor rests.'" (Luke 2:13–14). You might recognize this last line as *The Gloria*, an ancient Greek Christian hymn that was based on the words of these angels.

Saying "Yes" to God

The Annunciation is the feast of saying "yes" to God. This sentiment was expressed by Pope Francis during the March 25 feast celebrating the Archangel Gabriel's Annunciation to Mary (also known as Lady Day). The term "annunciation," in a non-religious context, simply means "an act or instance of announcing; a proclamation."

Pope Francis tells us that "when people do not want to say 'yes' to God, they usually do not say 'no,' they just hide like Adam and Eve did after they sinned." But after the sin of Adam and Eve, God did not give up on human beings. He continually reached out to holy men and women—from Abraham to Moses to the prophets—asking them to cooperate in his plan of salvation. God continues to say "yes" to human beings. The Gospel of Luke speaks to us of the end of that "yes" chain and the beginning of another with Mary's willingness to carry God's son. Pope Francis explains that "with this 'yes' God not only watches how humanity is proceeding ... he becomes one of us and takes on our flesh. Jesus himself is God's 'yes.'"

The feast of the Annunciation is a perfect time to think about our lives and whether we, like Mary, always say "yes" to God or whether we put our heads down, like Adam and Eve, pretending not to know what God is asking.

Pope Benedict XVI points out that the story of the Annunciation shows us how the Lord "knocks again and again at the door of the human heart." In Revelation 3:20, "he says to the 'angel' of the Church of Laodicea and, through him, to the people of all times: 'Behold, I stand at the door and knock; if any one hears my voice and opens the door, I will come in to him and eat with him, and he with me.'

"The Lord is at the door—at the door of the world and at the door of every individual heart. He knocks to be let in: the Incarnation of God, his taking flesh, must continue until the end of time. All must be reunited in Christ in one body: the great hymns on Christ in the Letters to the Ephesians and to the Colossians tell us this. Christ knocks. Today too he needs people who, so to speak, make their own flesh available to him, give him the matter of the world and of their lives, thus serving the unification between God and the world, until the reconciliation of the universe." Pope Benedict XVI tells us that by taking Christ into our lives, we bring God into the world, which leads to the salvation of all. Pope Benedict urges all of use to knock at people's hearts in Christ's Name. As we say "yes" to Christ, we are able to assume Gabriel's role: to bring Christ's call to all people.

Guardian Angel of the Holy Family

Tradition says Gabriel appeared to Saint Joseph on several occasions (Matthew 1 and 2). When Joseph discovered Mary was with child through the Holy Spirit, he decided to divorce her quietly. But "the angel of the Lord" appeared to him in a dream and explained that it was through the Holy Spirit that Mary conceived. The angel said, "She will bear a son and you are to name him Jesus, because he will save his people from their sins." The angel further told him that "they shall name him Emmanuel, which means "God is with us."(Matthew 1:23) So when Joseph awoke, he said "yes" and "took his wife into his home."

It was also Gabriel who appeared to Joseph to tell him to take Mary and Jesus to Egypt to protect them from Herod, who sought to kill the infant Jesus (Matthew 1:13–14).

Gabriel thus served as the guardian angel for the Holy Family, appearing to all of them at various times during the life and resurrection of Jesus.

Agony in Gethsemane

Though he is not mentioned by name, Gabriel is identified as the angel who consoled Jesus in the Garden of Gethsemane. Gethsemane is a garden at the foot of the Mount of Olives in Jerusalem. After the Last Supper, Jesus went there to pray as he prepared for his arrest and crucifixion. Jesus prayed, "Father, if you are willing, take this cup from me; yet not my will, but yours be done. And to strengthen him an angel from heaven appeared to him" (Luke 22:42–43). Just as he announced the miraculous birth of Jesus, Gabriel was present to offer him the strength of God in the garden.

Gabriel is often invoked to provide strength and comfort for those who are suffering, especially due to their faith. We can emulate Gabriel by sharing the strength and love of Jesus Christ with those who are in pain and by saying "yes" to God even when it may be inconvenient.

Final Judgment

Due to Gabriel's special role in announcing the Messiah, he is also believed to be the Archangel who will announce the Second Coming of Christ at the end of time. This prophesy is from 1 Thessalonians 4:16: "For the Lord himself will come down from heaven, with a loud command, with the voice of the archangel and with the trumpet call of God, and the dead in Christ will rise first."

Assumption of Mary

The Doctrine of the Assumption teaches that at the end of her life, the Virgin May was assumed body and soul into heaven. Catholics celebrate the Assumption on August 15 of each year. It was 1950 before the Catholic Church accepted the Virgin Mary's bodily assumption into heaven as official dogma, but the notion had long been part of her legend and a subject for artists. Much of the artwork depicts Gabriel as the angel who comes to tell Mary of the Assumption, just as he previously appeared to her, Joseph, and Jesus.

Various apocryphal books discuss Gabriel and the Assumption. One of these, the Book of Enoch, lists Gabriel and Michael as guardian angels of Israel. In the Book of Watchers, a section of Enoch about angels, Gabriel is listed as the fifth of five angels "who keep watch" (1 Enoch 20:7). Gabriel is also described as an angel "who is over Paradise and the serpents and the Cherubim." This book also counts Gabriel as an Archangel in two different lists. Enoch is not canonical, but many early theologians were aware of its content.

Angelic Rank

Gabriel is traditionally accepted as an Archangel, but this is not confirmed in the actual text of Scripture. Saint Raphael's assertion, "I am Raphael, one of the seven angels who stand and serve before the Glory of the Lord" (Tobit 12:15), coupled with Gabriel's words, "I am Gabriel, who stand before God" (Luke 1:19), indicate they are both God's messengers of the highest rank. The phrase "stand before God" is typically interpreted as a reference to one of the seven Archangels. The Orthodox Church also identifies Gabriel as one of the seven archangels.

As Gabriel was the messenger announcing one of the most important events in history, the coming of Our Savior, Jesus Christ, most scholars believe he would have to be an Archangel, or an angel of the highest rank. For all of these reasons, Gabriel's status as an archangel is commonly accepted.

Patron Saint

Gabriel is the Angel of the Annunciation and the Incarnation, the Angel of Consolation, and the Angel of Mercy. He is the bearer of good tidings and is often invoked as a comforter and helper. Because of the importance of the announcements from God he delivers, he is the patron of messengers and telecommunications. Today we have so much "noise" from the internet, social media, and other sources of information, it can be difficult to hear anything clearly. Devotion to Gabriel, who strengthens us with God's Good News, helps us hear what truly matters amidst the endless babbling of the media and internet.

Chapter 4:
Saint Raphael –
"God Heals"

Of the three Archangels named in Scripture, Raphael is perhaps the least well-known. Saint Raphael is the angel to whom is entrusted the task of healing. Pope Benedict XVI reminds us of the story of the Good Samaritan, who in accepting and healing the injured person lying on the side of the road becomes, without words, a witness of God's love. He points out that we are all this injured person, in need of being healed. Proclaiming the Gospel is always healing in itself, as we are all in need of truth and love above all things.

Raphael's focus is to help people grow closer to God, the source of all healing. Though he heals people physically, his primary mission is spiritual healing, such as overcoming attitudes and actions that hurt other people and move them further from God. He helps people admit and face their sins, confess, and turn to God, where true healing on every level can be found. While God provides the forgiveness we seek, it is also something we need to offer one another, as loving forgiveness is a form of healing.

Raphael is a companion who helps us find the courage to be honest and humble about our own sins and those of others. By helping us grow closer to God, he heals and strengthens our relationships to others, whether our connection to a stranger in need of acceptance or the bonds within our family or community. He helps heal the loneliness that a stranger or a traveler experiences and provides healing, protection, and companionship.

Interpreting the Book of Tobit

The United States Conference of Catholic Bishops points out that the Bible "conveys the Word of God in many literary forms." The Vatican said it is important to pay attention to literary forms, as the truth is presented in different forms of literary expression. Thus, the "interpreter must look for that meaning which the sacred writer intended to express and did in fact express through the medium of a contemporary literary form."

Written in the second century B.C., the Book of Tobit offered an example of how to manage the stress and difficulty of leading a pious Jewish life in a non-Jewish culture. Tobit illustrates that God does hear our prayers and notices our good works and that he answers us. The Conference states that the "message conveyed in these stories is not confined to one geographic place or historical period. It remains a valid expression of God's care for faithful people in every time and place."

The book also provides support to anyone who is struggling with the tension between evil and divine justice. Both Tobit and Sarah are pious, and the painful challenges they face seem to not make sense, as they lead good lives. In the long run, their faith and praise of God are rewarded. We can look at our lives the same way: we cannot know why bad things happen, but if we keep turning to God, we know that Jesus Christ was sent for our salvation and that in the long run, God will reward each of us with divine justice.

Much of what we know of Saint Raphael comes from the Book of Tobit. Known as a "biblical novella," Tobit is a didactic story that teaches about the ways of God, supporting people through challenging times, while also entertaining readers. The United Conference of Catholic Bishops describes such stories as "aids to the imagination" that contain "kernels of historical fact," but are primarily intended to "illustrate truths that transcend history." Tobit was pronounced canonical by the Council of Carthage in AD 397 and confirmed by the Council of Trent in 1546.

Tobias' Journey

In the Book of Tobit, the Archangel Raphael disguises himself as a man named Azariah and acts as both the companion and guide of Tobias and his dog. They set out on a journey to reclaim some money for Tobias' father, Tobit. Tobit is an elderly, pious Jew who buried murdered Jews in accordance with Jewish law but in defiance of the king. One evening, Tobit slept outside and was blinded by bird droppings. His blindness prevents Tobit from working, so he sends his son Tobias to a faraway town to reclaim some money he has in safekeeping.

In this faraway city, a beautiful woman named Sarah prays for death, as a demon named Asmodeus has killed all seven of her husbands on their wedding night before they can consummate the marriage. On the journey, Raphael tells Tobias he should marry Sarah, but Tobias is afraid that he, too, will be killed. As they rest by a lake, a monstrous fish tries to bite Tobias. They catch the fish, and Raphael directs Tobias to save its innards to use as medicine. When they arrive at Sarah's family home, Tobias marries her.

That night, Raphael instructs Tobias to burn the fish's organs. When the demon arrives to kill Tobias, the bitter smoke chases it away. Raphael pursues the demon and binds it in the desert. Raphael collects Tobit's money, and then the three of them and the dog return home. When Tobit comes out to greet his son, Raphael tells Tobias to put the fish's gall in Tobit's eyes, which cures his blindness.

When Tobit and Tobias try to give him half of the money in payment for his help, Raphael reveals himself to be an angel. He tells them, "I am the angel Raphael, one of the seven who stand before the Lord" (Tobit 12:15). While Scripture never explicitly names him as an Archangel, this is a phrase commonly understood to indicate an Archangel. When Raphael reveals himself as an Archangel, Tobit and Tobias are "greatly shaken" and fall to the ground in fear.

Raphael refuses to accept any thanks or payment; instead he tells them to direct all their thanks and praise to God, the

One who sent him. He explains that he was sent by God to bring healing to them and answer their prayer. Raphael says, "As far as I was concerned, when I was with you, my presence was not by any decision of mine, but by the will of God; he is the one whom you must bless as long as you live, he is the one that you must praise" (Tobit 12:18). He also explains that when Tobit and Sarah prayed, it was Raphael who "presented the record of your prayer before the Glory of the Lord," as well as when Tobit buried the dead. The entire family thanks God for "these marvelous works that God had done, because an angel of God appeared to them."

One of the most important things we discover about Raphael in Scripture is that he comes to us by the will of God and not by his own decision. By analogy, this can be applied to all of the Archangels and servants of God. Though they expect the respect a holy messenger deserves, they accept no credit or praise for themselves. All the glory, thanks, and praise is referred back to God, who sent them.

Strengthening Relationships

Pope Benedict XVI teaches us that the Book of Tobit illustrates the Archangel Raphael's emblematic task of healing: "He heals the disturbed communion between a man and a woman. He heals their love. He drives out the demons who over and over again exhaust and destroy their love. He purifies the atmosphere between the two and gives them the ability to accept each other for ever.

"In the New Testament, the order of marriage established in creation and threatened in many ways by sin, is healed through Christ's acceptance of it in his redeeming love. He makes marriage a sacrament: his love, put on a cross for us, is the healing power which in all forms of chaos offers the capacity for reconciliation, purifies the atmosphere and mends the wounds." Raphael is the messenger of the redeeming love of Christ. Through Christ, all sins are forgiven, and with this cleansing, we can forgive and rejuvenate all our relationships in love.

In the Book of Tobit, we see all manner of relationships that are healed through God's love. Tobit's relationship with his family is restored, Tobias and Sarah are married and form a new family after Sarah is healed, Tobias reaches out to members of the community through marriage and his journey. Christ is the healing that allows us to have loving relationships with one another.

Vision

The Book of Tobit speaks of the healing of sightless eyes. While Raphael heals Tobit's physical blindness, Pope Benedict XVI points out other types of blindness that are just as painful: "We all know how threatened we are today by blindness to God. How great is the danger that with all we know of material things and can do with them, we become blind to God's light. Healing this blindness through the message of faith and the witness of love is Raphael's service." Again we are reminded that the Archangels are messengers of God's love and that all they bring us comes from God.

We can emulate this healing of blindness by seeing things as they are from God's perspective, rather than our own. Though we are able to ask God for what we would like, ultimately he knows the best path. Sometimes that path is long or difficult, but it is made less so with the knowledge that he is always waiting for us at the end of any journey.

Forms of Healing

The Old Testament is not the only place we can find Saint Raphael in the Scriptures. Many Church Fathers believe that Raphael is mentioned in the Gospel of John, which speaks of a pool called Bethesda, where the sick were brought for healing. "An angel of the Lord descended at certain times into the pond; and the water was moved. And he that went down first into the pond after the motion of the water was made whole of whatsoever infirmity he lay under" (John

5:1–4). While he is not mentioned by name, Raphael's penchant for healing makes it likely this is also his work.

Raphael's name can be translated as "Medicine of God," "Healing power of God," or simply, "God heals." Some people have even translated it as "Ointment of God." His name may be derived from the Hebrew word *rophe*, which means "doctor." The Hebrew word *rophe* (or *rapha*) means "to restore," "to heal," or "to make beautiful." Raphael is traditionally associated with the Sacrament of Penance, as Confession and forgiveness are aspects of healing.

Like the healing Raphael provides in Tobit, the word *rophe* addresses not just physical health, but also all other states of healing—the renewal of broken hearts, spirits, souls, *and* bodies. For example, Isaiah 53:5 speaks about the salvation Jesus offer us: "He was pierced for our sins, crushed for our iniquity. He bore the punishment that makes us whole, by his wounds we were healed." In this passage, the word "healed" is *rophe*, and we see that it refers to the healing Christ brings through his sacrifice. As the angels are God's messengers, the message of Christ's healing is emphasized through their work. In this way, Raphael helps bring us closer to God to experience the peace and love that God wants to provide.

Apocryphal Works

In addition to canonical Scripture, Raphael also appears in a number of Jewish and Christian apocryphal sources, such as the Book of Enoch. Apocryphal sources are not part of the Bible, and so are not considered inspired, but they can be interesting as historical literature.

Raphael appears in the Book of Enoch, an ancient Jewish text, where he is depicted as a healer, as he is commanded by God to "heal" the earth when it is defiled by the sins of the fallen angels. In verse 10:10, God tells Raphael: "Restore the earth, which the [fallen] angels have corrupted; and announce life to it, that I may revive it." Enoch's guide tells us that Raphael "presides over every suffering and every affliction" on earth and Raphael's mission from God is to provide healing, restoration, and comfort. In 1 Enoch 20:7 we find a description of "Raphael, one of the holy angels, who is over spirits of men." In Enoch 40:9, Raphael is described as one "who is set over all the diseases and all the wounds of the children of men." He also binds a demon named Azazel under a desert called Dudael in Enoch 10:4–6.

Raphael also appears in the Zohar, a religious text in the mystical Jewish faith Kabbalah. In Genesis chapter 23, Raphael is "appointed to heal the earth of its evil and affliction and the maladies of mankind." The Babylonian Talmud identifies Raphael as one of three angels who appear to Abraham in the oak grove of Mamre. The mission of Raphael, who appears there with Michael and Gabriel, is to heal Abraham from his circumcision and save Lot.

Patron Saint

Raphael is the patron saint of travelers due to the valuable help he provides Tobias on their journey. Thanks to Raphael, Tobias gains knowledge, valuable experiences, and a beautiful and pious wife. Raphael is invoked for journeys and at critical junctures in life. He is also the patron saint of the blind, happy meetings, nurses, physicians, guilds of healing, marriage, young people, and Catholic studies.

In Catholic Europe, he was a special protector of sailors; at Venice's famous Doge's Palace, there is a plaque that depicts Raphael with Tobias, who holds a scroll that reads: *Efficia fretum quietum* ("Keep the Gulf quiet"). On July 8, 1497, when Vasco da Gama set sail from Lisbon to sail to India, the flagship was named—at the king of Portugal's request—the *St. Raphael.* When they reached the Cape of Good Hope safely, they placed a small column in Raphael's honor. The small statue of Raphael that accompanied the ship is on display in the Navy Museum in Lisbon.

As he is known for acts of healing, mercy, and clarity, we can emulate Raphael by aiding those who are ill or homeless. We can provide comfort, companionship, and community to the traveler and the migrant, whether their journeys be physical or spiritual. Whether it is praying for them, volunteering with organizations that embody these values, or simply reaching out with God's love to others, we can also be healing messengers of God's love, which unites us all in community.

Chapter 5:
Apocryphal Archangels

While Roman (or Latin) Catholics only venerate the three Archangels mentioned in Scripture—Michael, Gabriel, and Raphael—plus our guardian angels, Eastern (or Byzantine) Catholics venerate all seven by name. Eastern Catholics are generally "in union with the Bishop of Rome," but embrace some customs, traditions, and liturgical rites that differ from the Roman rite.

The Holy See's 2002 Directory on Popular Piety and the Liturgy does state "[t]he practice of assigning names to the Holy Angels should be discouraged, except in the cases of Gabriel, Raphael and Michael whose names are contained in Holy Scripture." However, another important part of the Directory says that judgments on matters of popular piety, such as venerating angels by name, are "for the diocesan Bishop or for the Bishops of a given territory in which such forms are found" to determine. Bishops "should take a positive and encouraging stance with regard to popular religiosity, unless there are patently obvious reasons to the contrary."

The Directory's main focus is on ensuring that the Liturgy is the center of the Church's life and is not substituted or "placed on par with any other form of religious expression." Popular devotional practices "naturally culminate" in the celebration of the Liturgy and encourage people to be enthusiastic about their spiritual life and interested in attending Mass.

This means traditions that differ from the Roman rite, such as the Eastern Catholic tradition, are allowed to take their historical and cultural practices into account. So, venerating all seven Archangels by name, even though those names come from apocryphal sources, is acceptable as long as it is directed toward enriching the Liturgy (Mass) and the individual's connection to God.

It is not in itself forbidden to refer to names from apocryphal sources. For example, the Church takes the names of the three wise men, Mary's parents, and the feast of Mary's presentation in the temple from apocryphal sources. These are simply illustrations of the Church acknowledging tradition. Devotional practices that encourage dedication to God, such as the rosary, while not doctrine, are seen as positive and fostering a closer connection to him. It is only when a devotion distracts from this relationship that it is found to be unproductive and, thus, discouraged.

Canonical and Apocryphal Books

Another reason Roman Catholics do not venerate all seven archangels by name, but Eastern Catholics do, is because the latter recognize different Old Testament books as canonical. The Eastern Orthodox and Catholic Churches use the Septuagint Old Testament, though there are some variations between the Greek and Slavonic versions. The Septuagint is the translation of the Hebrew Bible into Greek—it is the oldest translation of the Old Testament into another language. Assembled from a collection of Greek translations produced by many people over a few hundred years, it was preferred to the Hebrew version by the early Christian church.

While all Christians agree that the books in the Bible are the inspired Word of God, we disagree about which books belong in the canonical Bible. For Catholics, the Old Testament writings that were not included in the Bible are referred to as "apocryphal."

New Testament authors did sometimes quote these writings. For instance, Saint Jude refers to a fight between the Archangel Michael and the devil over the body of Moses (Jude 9). The Church Fathers explain these references in a variety of ways. For instance, Origen says these references occurred "under Divine inspiration." Saint Jerome states that the New Testament authors did not necessarily approve of an entire work that they mentioned. Saint Augustine says that there may be some truths in these books, but their "origin was not clear to the Fathers" and "they have no canonical authority owing to their large admixture of error." Also, many of these apocryphal works were very popular at a given time and widely read, so the

Church Fathers needed to emphasize the focus on canonical Scripture as the authority.

There are many apocryphal books that contain the names of angels beyond the three we find in Scripture. These sources vary wildly in terms of which names are mentioned, and various traditions embrace many different names. Sometimes the names depend upon the source; other times they depend upon the translation or other factors. As a result, there are a wide variety of names that appear to refer to the same angel. Though it can be a bit confusing, and the names of the four Archangels not mentioned in Scripture vary according to tradition, it is still useful to consider a few of these apocryphal works and some of the attributes of the other four Archangels.

Book of Esdras

This book is an example of apocryphal books changing names and numbers; it is definitely one of the more confusing examples. Four books are attributed to the prophet Esdras (also spelled Ezra). They became known by some as 1, 2, 3, and 4 Esdras.

In some traditions, the Books of 1 and 2 Esdras were renamed to Ezra and Nehemiah, which are canonical books of the Catholic and Protestant Old Testament. Then, 3 and 4 Esdras became known as 1 and 2 Esdras. If you look in an older Catholic Bible, you can find the Books of Ezra and Nehemiah labeled as 1 and 2 Esdras, though newer translations refer to them as Ezra and Nehemiah.

Accordingly, the last two books attributed to this prophet are sometimes called 3 and 4 Esdras, and sometimes 1 and 2 Esdras. Neither of these two books is accepted by Protestants or Catholics. However, some Eastern Orthodox Churches accept one or the other of these books.

Book of Enoch

The Book of Enoch is an ancient Jewish work, ascribed by tradition to Enoch, but is only viewed as canonical by the Ethiopian and Eritrean Orthodox Churches. It is a combination of at least five different works, dating from different time periods. The first book, called the Book of the Watchers, has the largest number of angelic mentions. This book describes how fallen angels mated with human women and their children were known as Nephilim. Both Jewish and Christian sources have tremendous disagreement about what these stories might mean. The work is based on a common theme in early Christian literature, that of a holy man or prophet—Enoch—describing his journey through a supernatural world.

The book describes the world before the Flood. It describes beings known as "Watchers" (or Shomerim") that give Enoch a tour of the underworld, where he encounters the Tree of Life and the Tree of Knowledge. The Archangels Michael, Uriel, Raphael, and Gabriel are all mentioned as noticing the sinfulness and war upon the earth (though different translations include the name Suriel). These angels in heaven complain about the exploits of fallen angels, such as Azazel and Semjaza. God gives each of the Archangels a mission to deal with the havoc caused by the fallen angels. Enoch then describes the "holy angels who watch," listing Uriel, Raphael, Raguel, Michael, Saraqael, Gabriel and Remiel. Enoch also describes Seraphim, Cherubim, and Ophanim. Michael, Raphael, Gabriel, and Phanuel are listed as "holy angels" who surround the house of God and "go in and out of that house."

The Book of Enoch was widely read, and many Church Fathers believed Enoch was an important prophet. There are also mentions of stories from the Book of Enoch that appear in canonical Scripture. For instance, in some translations of the Book of Daniel, we see the term "watcher" used to indicate an angel. This is the only place in the Bible that term is used, though it is common in extra-canonical Jewish literature, such as Enoch. Daniel 4:10 reads: "In the vision I saw while in bed, a holy watcher came down from heaven...." The New American Bible (Revised Edition) includes a footnote that "a holy watcher" can be literally translated as "a watcher and a holy one," which are two terms for angels.

Another reference to the Book of Enoch in Scripture is found in the Epistle of Saint Jude. This book is one of the earliest Christian texts to give an Archangel a proper name, when he describes a fight between the Archangel Michael and the devil: "Yet the archangel Michael, when he argued with the devil in a dispute over the body of Moses, did not venture to pronounce a reviling judgment upon him but said, 'May the Lord rebuke you!'" (Jude 9).

Names of the Other Four Archangels

The names of the other Archangels are found in Hebrew non-canonical works like Esdras 3 and 4 or are named in the writings of Church Fathers. The names of the non-scriptural Archangels exhibit a tremendous amount of variety, with a multitude of different lists and spellings. While we cannot determine an "official" or complete list, it is interesting to look at some of the scholarship and consider the positive attributes of these Archangels, even if we cannot know their names for certain.

In order to explore the attributes of the other Archangels, we need to decide upon a single list from the many that exist. The earliest Christian references are in the early sixth century; Church Fathers from Pope Saint Gregory to Pseudo-Dionysius all compiled lists of the seven Archangels. Each of these lists included the three mentioned in Scripture—Michael, Gabriel, and Raphael.

Keeping in mind the great variety of names, there is a devotional tradition of associating the seven Archangels with the seven Sacraments of the Church. This is not doctrine, but provides a list of names for us to explore. According to one tradition, the list of Archangels includes Michael, Gabriel, Raphael, Uriel, Raguel, Zerachiel, and Remiel. They are associated with the following Sacraments: Michael is the Patron of the Sacrament of the Holy Eucharist; Gabriel is the Patron of the Sacrament of Baptism; Raphael is the Patron of the Sacrament of Reconciliation; Uriel is the Patron of the Sacrament of Confirmation; Raguel is the Patron of the Sacrament of Holy Orders; Zerachiel is the Patron of the Sacrament of Matrimony; and Remiel is the Patron of the Sacrament of the Anointing of the Sick.

None of these concepts is doctrine, and the Sacraments do not flow from the Archangels; they only come from Christ. However, the Archangels can inspire us and help us think deeply about the Sacraments and the amazing gifts God has bestowed upon us.

Uriel

Uriel's name means "Fire of God," "God is my Light," or "Enlightener." He reveals divine knowledge and is often depicted holding a flame. He is the patron saint of the arts, the Sacrament of Confirmation, and poetry.

Uriel plays an important role in apocryphal writings such as the Book of Enoch, the Apocalypse of Peter, and 2 Baruch, though currently none of these books is canonical in the Roman Church. Uriel was traditionally quite popular in both Jewish and Christian history, and many Jewish scholars and Christian Church Fathers found these texts credible. There are many stories regarding Uriel as a messenger of education and divine knowledge we receive from God. For example, in the apocryphal Book of Esdras, the prophet Ezra asks God questions and Uriel is sent by God to teach him.

In other writings, there is a story of Uriel rescuing John the Baptist from King Herod's Massacre of Innocents. Uriel carries John and his mother Elizabeth to join Mary, Joseph, and Jesus after they flee to Egypt. This reunion is depicted in Leonardo da Vinci's *Virgin of the Rocks* (1483–1486). In the version held by the Louvre, Mary is in the center of the composition, with her right hand around the baby Jesus. On the right side, below Mary, we see Uriel and the baby Saint

John the Baptist. Uriel sits protectively next to him, and both of them are pointing at Jesus. Uriel looks out to make eye contact with the view, inviting us into the knowledge of the salvation the Christ Child brings. Uriel's billowing red cloak—perhaps a reference to his name, "Fire of God"—captures the eye, as the background of the painting is mostly mottled grey and brown, rock and earth.

Uriel is mentioned in the Book of Enoch as one of the "holy angels who watch." Uriel watches over the world and "over Tartarus." Tartarus is an abyss in Greek mythology where the dead are judged; it is likely this is a reference to something similar to hell. Other apocryphal sources say he is God's steward, or "watcher," over Sheol/Hades (hell). Traditionally, he is considered to be the Archangel of repentance and of the damned.

Raguel

Raguel's name means "Friend of God." Depending on the source, this angel is also known as Sealtiel, Sakuel, or Saphiel. Traditionally, he is revered as the Archangel of justice or fairness. He is associated with justice, fairness, and redemption.

Jewish and Christian traditions tend to agree that Raguel is an enforcer of laws—he keeps fallen angels (demons) in line and punishes those who exceed their boundaries. He can destroy evil spirits and cast them into hell. His focus is on protecting the minds of humans from demonic influence and temptation. Some traditions believe he is the angel who separates the souls of the faithful from the unfaithful.

Raguel is mentioned in the Book of Enoch as one of the "holy angels who watch." Raguel is a watcher "who takes vengeance on the world of the luminaries" who defy God's laws. Raguel is also named as one of the Archangels who carries Enoch as a human to and from heaven.

Zerachiel

Zerachiel's name means "God's command." This Archangel is known by a large number of different names. In some translations of the Book of Enoch, he is named Saraqael. Depending on the source, this angel is also known as Saraqael, Barachiel, Selaphiel, Zerachiel, Selapheal, Salathiel, Selathiel, Sealteal, Seraphiel, Sarakiel, Sariel, Suriel, Suriyel, and Saraqael.

There is much disagreement not just about the name, but also about the attributes of this angel. For instance, one alternate name for Zerachiel, Saraqael, is referred to as a heavenly angel who looks over those "who sin in spirit," yet in Enoch, he is also listed as one of the fallen angels. So not only do the different books conflict; there is conflict even within a single book.

Traditionally, he is revered as the Archangel of God's judgment. He is described as leading souls to judgment.

The various names of this angel are associated with slightly different traditions. Again, there are many angels named in apocryphal books, and we do not know if they are accurate. A look at a couple of variations illustrates the very different attributes associated with any selected name for this angel.

As Barachiel, his name means "Blessed by God." He is often depicted with a white rose against his chest, or with rose petals, signifying God's blessings. He distributes blessings earned through good deeds. Similarly, sometimes he is seen with a bread basket or staff, symbolizing children as a gift from God. In the Eastern tradition, he is a patron of family and married life. He is described as leader of the guardian angels. He appears in the Book of Enoch, described as the leader of 496,000 angels and as one of the angels who guard God's throne. He is an official saint of the Eastern Church. Traditionally, he has dominion over lightening and storms.

As Selaphiel, his name means "the prayer of God" or "one who prays to God." He is the angel of prayer, assisting people in connecting to God and in praying intently. He is often depicted holding a vessel of water and two fish, representative of God's bounty that comes through prayer. Selaphiel appears by name in the apocryphal *The Conflict of Adam and Eve*, where God directs him to save Adam and Eve from Satan after they are expelled from Eden. He is the official saint of prayer for the Eastern Church and was traditionally venerated as the patron saint of prayer in the Roman Church.

Remiel

While Roman (or Latin) Catholics only venerate the three Archangels mentioned in Scripture—Michael, Gabriel, and Raphael—plus our guardian angels, Eastern (or Byzantine) Catholics venerate all seven by name. Eastern Catholics are generally "in union with the Bishop of Rome," but embrace some customs, traditions, and liturgical rites that differ from the Roman rite.

The Holy See's 2002 Directory on Popular Piety and the Liturgy does state "[t]he practice of assigning names to the Holy Angels should be discouraged, except in the cases of Gabriel, Raphael and Michael whose names are contained in Holy Scripture." However, another important part of the

Directory says that judgments on matters of popular piety, such as venerating angels by name, are "for the diocesan Bishop or for the Bishops of a given territory in which such forms are found" to determine. Bishops "should take a positive and encouraging stance with regard to popular religiosity, unless there are patently obvious reasons to the contrary."

The Directory's main focus is on ensuring that the Liturgy is the center of the Church's life and is not substituted or "placed on par with any other form of religious expression." Popular devotional practices "naturally culminate" in the celebration of the Liturgy and encourage people to be enthusiastic about their spiritual life and interested in attending Mass.

This means traditions that differ from the Roman rite, such as the Eastern Catholic tradition, are allowed to take their historical and cultural practices into account. So, venerating all seven Archangels by name, even though those names come from apocryphal sources, is acceptable as long as it is directed toward enriching the Liturgy (Mass) and the individual's connection to God.

It is not in itself forbidden to refer to names from apocryphal sources. For example, the Church takes the names of the three wise men, Mary's parents, and the feast of Mary's presentation in the temple from apocryphal sources. These are simply illustrations of the Church acknowledging tradition. Devotional practices that encourage dedication to God, such as the rosary, while not doctrine, are seen as positive and fostering a closer connection to him. It is only when a devotion distracts from this relationship that it is found to be unproductive and, thus, discouraged.

Canonical and Apocryphal Books

Another reason Roman Catholics do not venerate all seven archangels by name, but Eastern Catholics do, is because the latter recognize different Old Testament books as canonical. The Eastern Orthodox and Catholic Churches use the Septuagint Old Testament, though there are some variations between the Greek and Slavonic versions. The Septuagint is the translation of the Hebrew Bible into Greek—it is the oldest translation of the Old Testament into another language. Assembled from a collection of Greek translations produced by many people over a few hundred years, it was preferred to the Hebrew version by the early Christian church.

While all Christians agree that the books in the Bible are the inspired Word of God, we disagree about which books belong in the canonical Bible. For Catholics, the Old

Testament writings that were not included in the Bible are referred to as "apocryphal."

New Testament authors did sometimes quote these writings. For instance, Saint Jude refers to a fight between the Archangel Michael and the devil over the body of Moses (Jude 9). The Church Fathers explain these references in a variety of ways. For instance, Origen says these references occurred "under Divine inspiration." Saint Jerome states that the New Testament authors did not necessarily approve of an entire work that they mentioned. Saint Augustine says that there may be some truths in these books, but their "origin was not clear to the Fathers" and "they have no canonical authority owing to their large admixture of error." Also, many of these apocryphal works were very popular at a given time and widely read, so the Church Fathers needed to emphasize the focus on canonical Scripture as the authority.

There are many apocryphal books that contain the names of angels beyond the three we find in Scripture. These sources vary wildly in terms of which names are mentioned, and various traditions embrace many different names. Sometimes the names depend upon the source; other times they depend upon the translation or other factors. As a result, there are a wide variety of names that appear to refer to the same angel. Though it can be a bit confusing, and the names of the four Archangels not mentioned in

Scripture vary according to tradition, it is still useful to consider a few of these apocryphal works and some of the attributes of the other four Archangels.

Book of Esdras

This book is an example of apocryphal books changing names and numbers; it is definitely one of the more confusing examples. Four books are attributed to the prophet Esdras (also spelled Ezra). They became known by some as 1, 2, 3, and 4 Esdras.

In some traditions, the Books of 1 and 2 Esdras were renamed to Ezra and Nehemiah, which are canonical books of the Catholic and Protestant Old Testament. Then, 3 and 4 Esdras became known as 1 and 2 Esdras. If you look in an older Catholic Bible, you can find the Books of Ezra and Nehemiah labeled as 1 and 2 Esdras, though newer translations refer to them as Ezra and Nehemiah.

Accordingly, the last two books attributed to this prophet are sometimes called 3 and 4 Esdras, and sometimes 1 and 2 Esdras. Neither of these two books is accepted by Protestants or Catholics. However, some Eastern Orthodox Churches accept one or the other of these books.

Book of Enoch

The Book of Enoch is an ancient Jewish work, ascribed by tradition to Enoch, but is only viewed as canonical by the Ethiopian and Eritrean Orthodox Churches. It is a combination of at least five different works, dating from different time periods. The first book, called the Book of the Watchers, has the largest number of angelic mentions. This book describes how fallen angels mated with human women and their children were known as Nephilim. Both Jewish and Christian sources have tremendous disagreement about what these stories might mean. The work is based on a common theme in early Christian literature, that of a holy man or prophet—Enoch—describing his journey through a supernatural world.

The book describes the world before the Flood. It describes beings known as "Watchers" (or Shomerim") that give Enoch a tour of the underworld, where he encounters the Tree of Life and the Tree of Knowledge. The Archangels Michael, Uriel, Raphael, and Gabriel are all mentioned as noticing the sinfulness and war upon the earth (though different translations include the name Suriel). These angels in heaven complain about the exploits of fallen angels, such as Azazel and Semjaza. God gives each of the Archangels a mission to deal with the havoc caused by the fallen angels. Enoch then describes the "holy angels who watch," listing Uriel, Raphael, Raguel, Michael, Saraqael,

Gabriel and Remiel. Enoch also describes Seraphim, Cherubim, and Ophanim. Michael, Raphael, Gabriel, and Phanuel are listed as "holy angels" who surround the house of God and "go in and out of that house."

The Book of Enoch was widely read, and many Church Fathers believed Enoch was an important prophet. There are also mentions of stories from the Book of Enoch that appear in canonical Scripture. For instance, in some translations of the Book of Daniel, we see the term "watcher" used to indicate an angel. This is the only place in the Bible that term is used, though it is common in extra-canonical Jewish literature, such as Enoch. Daniel 4:10 reads: "In the vision I saw while in bed, a holy watcher came down from heaven...." The New American Bible (Revised Edition) includes a footnote that "a holy watcher" can be literally translated as "a watcher and a holy one," which are two terms for angels.

Another reference to the Book of Enoch in Scripture is found in the Epistle of Saint Jude. This book is one of the earliest Christian texts to give an Archangel a proper name, when he describes a fight between the Archangel Michael and the devil: "Yet the archangel Michael, when he argued with the devil in a dispute over the body of Moses, did not venture to pronounce a reviling judgment upon him but said, 'May the Lord rebuke you!'" (Jude 9).

Names of the Other Four Archangels

The names of the other Archangels are found in Hebrew non-canonical works like Esdras 3 and 4 or are named in the writings of Church Fathers. The names of the non-scriptural Archangels exhibit a tremendous amount of variety, with a multitude of different lists and spellings. While we cannot determine an "official" or complete list, it is interesting to look at some of the scholarship and consider the positive attributes of these Archangels, even if we cannot know their names for certain.

In order to explore the attributes of the other Archangels, we need to decide upon a single list from the many that exist. The earliest Christian references are in the early sixth century; Church Fathers from Pope Saint Gregory to Pseudo-Dionysius all compiled lists of the seven Archangels. Each of these lists included the three mentioned in Scripture—Michael, Gabriel, and Raphael.

Keeping in mind the great variety of names, there is a devotional tradition of associating the seven Archangels with the seven Sacraments of the Church. This is not doctrine, but provides a list of names for us to explore. According to one tradition, the list of Archangels includes Michael, Gabriel, Raphael, Uriel, Raguel, Zerachiel, and Remiel. They are associated with the following Sacraments:

Michael is the Patron of the Sacrament of the Holy Eucharist; Gabriel is the Patron of the Sacrament of Baptism; Raphael is the Patron of the Sacrament of Reconciliation; Uriel is the Patron of the Sacrament of Confirmation; Raguel is the Patron of the Sacrament of Holy Orders; Zerachiel is the Patron of the Sacrament of Matrimony; and Remiel is the Patron of the Sacrament of the Anointing of the Sick.

None of these concepts is doctrine, and the Sacraments do not flow from the Archangels; they only come from Christ. However, the Archangels can inspire us and help us think deeply about the Sacraments and the amazing gifts God has bestowed upon us.

Uriel

Uriel's name means "Fire of God," "God is my Light," or "Enlightener." He reveals divine knowledge and is often depicted holding a flame. He is the patron saint of the arts, the Sacrament of Confirmation, and poetry.

Uriel plays an important role in apocryphal writings such as the Book of Enoch, the Apocalypse of Peter, and 2 Baruch, though currently none of these books is canonical in the Roman Church. Uriel was traditionally quite popular in both

Jewish and Christian history, and many Jewish scholars and Christian Church Fathers found these texts credible. There are many stories regarding Uriel as a messenger of education and divine knowledge we receive from God. For example, in the apocryphal Book of Esdras, the prophet Ezra asks God questions and Uriel is sent by God to teach him.

In other writings, there is a story of Uriel rescuing John the Baptist from King Herod's Massacre of Innocents. Uriel carries John and his mother Elizabeth to join Mary, Joseph, and Jesus after they flee to Egypt. This reunion is depicted in Leonardo da Vinci's Virgin of the Rocks (1483–1486). In the version held by the Louvre, Mary is in the center of the composition, with her right hand around the baby Jesus. On the right side, below Mary, we see Uriel and the baby Saint John the Baptist. Uriel sits protectively next to him, and both of them are pointing at Jesus. Uriel looks out to make eye contact with the view, inviting us into the knowledge of the salvation the Christ Child brings. Uriel's billowing red cloak—perhaps a reference to his name, "Fire of God"—captures the eye, as the background of the painting is mostly mottled grey and brown, rock and earth.

Uriel is mentioned in the Book of Enoch as one of the "holy angels who watch." Uriel watches over the world and "over Tartarus." Tartarus is an abyss in Greek mythology where the dead are judged; it is likely this is a reference to something similar to hell. Other apocryphal sources say he is God's steward, or "watcher," over Sheol/Hades (hell). Traditionally, he is considered to be the Archangel of repentance and of the damned.

Raguel

Raguel's name means "Friend of God." Depending on the source, this angel is also known as Sealtiel, Sakuel, or Saphiel. Traditionally, he is revered as the Archangel of justice or fairness. He is associated with justice, fairness, and redemption.

Jewish and Christian traditions tend to agree that Raguel is an enforcer of laws—he keeps fallen angels (demons) in line and punishes those who exceed their boundaries. He can destroy evil spirits and cast them into hell. His focus is on protecting the minds of humans from demonic influence and temptation. Some traditions believe he is the angel who separates the souls of the faithful from the unfaithful.

Raguel is mentioned in the Book of Enoch as one of the "holy angels who watch." Raguel is a watcher "who takes vengeance on the world of the luminaries" who defy God's laws. Raguel is also named as one of the Archangels who carries Enoch as a human to and from heaven.

Zerachiel

Zerachiel's name means "God's command." This Archangel is known by a large number of different names. In some translations of the Book of Enoch, he is named Saraqael. Depending on the source, this angel is also known as Saraqael, Barachiel, Selaphiel, Zerachiel, Selapheal, Salathiel, Selathiel, Sealteal, Seraphiel, Sarakiel, Sariel, Suriel, Suriyel, and Saraqael.

There is much disagreement not just about the name, but also about the attributes of this angel. For instance, one alternate name for Zerachiel, Saraqael, is referred to as a heavenly angel who looks over those "who sin in spirit," yet in Enoch, he is also listed as one of the fallen angels. So not only do the different books conflict; there is conflict even within a single book.

Traditionally, he is revered as the Archangel of God's judgment. He is described as leading souls to judgment.

The various names of this angel are associated with slightly different traditions. Again, there are many angels named in apocryphal books, and we do not know if they are accurate.

A look at a couple of variations illustrates the very different attributes associated with any selected name for this angel.

As Barachiel, his name means "Blessed by God." He is often depicted with a white rose against his chest, or with rose petals, signifying God's blessings. He distributes blessings earned through good deeds. Similarly, sometimes he is seen with a bread basket or staff, symbolizing children as a gift from God. In the Eastern tradition, he is a patron of family and married life. He is described as leader of the guardian angels. He appears in the Book of Enoch, described as the leader of 496,000 angels and as one of the angels who guard God's throne. He is an official saint of the Eastern Church. Traditionally, he has dominion over lightening and storms.

As Selaphiel, his name means "the prayer of God" or "one who prays to God." He is the angel of prayer, assisting people in connecting to God and in praying intently. He is often depicted holding a vessel of water and two fish, representative of God's bounty that comes through prayer. Selaphiel appears by name in the apocryphal The Conflict of Adam and Eve, where God directs him to save Adam and Eve from Satan after they are expelled from Eden. He is the official saint of prayer for the Eastern Church and was traditionally venerated as the patron saint of prayer in the Roman Church.

Remiel

Remiel's name means "Thunder of God," "Mercy of God," "God uplifts," or "Compassion of God." Traditionally, he is revered as the Archangel of hope and faith. He is the patron saint of the Sacrament of Anointing of the Sick. Some traditions say he guides faithful souls to heaven.

Some translations of the Book of Enoch say Remiel is a fallen angel who took a human wife. However, Remiel is also listed in Enoch as one of the "holy angels who watch" and is described as one "whom God set over those who rise." Some argue that the entire story is incorrect.

There is also an Archangel named Jeremiel in Esdras, which may be Judiel or Uriel under another name. This angel may also be known as Jerahmeel, Jehudiel, or Jeremiel.

In 2 Baruch 55:3, he "presides over true visions." He is said to provide instructions from God to the other seven Archangels, and he encourages working for the glory of God. The Eastern Church considers him a patron saint of human governance; leaders of all sorts, judges, and others pray to him for guidance.

As Jeremiel, he is recognized as an archangel in Esdras and by the Orthodox Church as one of the seven Archangels. The Orthodox Church recognizes this Book of Esdras as canonical.

There is also an Archangel named Jeremiel in Esdras, which may be Judiel or Uriel under another name. This angel may also be known as Jerahmeel, Jehudiel, or Jeremiel.

In 2 Baruch 55:3, he "presides over true visions." He is said to provide instructions from God to the other seven Archangels, and he encourages working for the glory of God. The Eastern Church considers him a patron saint of human governance; leaders of all sorts, judges, and others pray to him for guidance.

As Jeremiel, he is recognized as an archangel in Esdras and by the Orthodox Church as one of the seven Archangels. The Orthodox Church recognizes this Book of Esdras as canonical.

Chapter 6:
Angelic Devotion and Prayer

According to the Directory for Popular Piety in 2002, devotion to the Holy Angels enhances Christian life in certain ways: First, it creates "devout gratitude to God for having placed these heavenly spirits of great sanctity and dignity at the service of man." Second, it fosters "an attitude of devotion deriving from the knowledge of living constantly in the presence of the Holy Angels of God," which offers us "serenity and confidence in facing difficult situations, since the Lord guides and protects the faithful in the way of justice through the ministry of His Holy Angels." Devotions and prayer are some of the ways we can "talk" to angels.

Angels and the Liturgy

The Church encourages devotion to the holy angels and reaffirmed this tradition in the 2002 Directory for Popular Piety. The Liturgy and popular devotions are two different forms of worship that have a synergistic relationship to one another. However, the Liturgy remains the primary point of worship so as to "clearly and prudently… channel the yearnings of prayer and the charismatic life" found in devotions. Popular devotions, due to their "symbolic and expressive qualities, can often provide the Liturgy with important insights for enculturation and stimulate an effective" and dynamic creativity.

The Liturgy celebrates angels in many different ways. At Mass we repeat the words the angels gave us to praise the thrice-holy God: "Holy, Holy, Holy, is the Lord God of Hosts!" (Isaiah 6:3). Angels, especially the Archangel Michael, are invoked during the Church's funeral liturgy, *In Paradisum deducant te angeli*, with the words "May the angels lead you into paradise." The "Cherubic Hymn" of the Byzantine Liturgy celebrates the angels Saint Michael, Saint Raphael, and Saint Gabriel, and the guardian angels. Through the combination of Mass and devotions, the Church affirms faith in angels, asking for help and protection.

Doctrine of Intercession

The Catholic practice of intercession, or asking saints and angels to pray for us, is often misunderstood. Whenever we petition an angel or saint, it is a request that they pray to God for us. For instance, when we pray the Hail Mary, we ask, "Pray for us sinners." Intercession requires the understanding that "all benefit, aid and prayers we receive from angels and saints are benefits we receive from God, through His Son Jesus Christ our Lord, Who alone is our Redeemer and Savior."

The Catechism of the Catholic Church points out that praying for one another has always been an important component of loving others. "Since Abraham, intercession—asking on behalf of another—has been characteristic of a heart attuned to God's mercy. In the age of the Church, Christian intercession participates in Christ's, as an expression of the communion of saints. In intercession, he who prays looks 'not only to his own interests, but also to the interests of others,' even to the point of praying for those who do him harm."

Scripture supports prayers for and from our "brothers," whether they be saints, angels, or other humans. The offering of "supplications, prayers, petitions and thanksgivings" is "good and pleasing to God our Savior" (1 Timothy 2:1–4). Scripture also tells us that the angels play a role in bringing our prayers to God: "The smoke of the incense along with the prayers of the holy ones went up before God from the hand of the angel" (Revelation 8:4). All the souls in heaven, the people on earth and those in purgatory, are "one mystical body, with Christ for their head." We are reminded of this connection to one another in Matthew 25:40, where Jesus says, "Truly I tell you, whatever you did for one of the least of these brothers and sisters of mine, you did for me."

Jesus told us the greatest of all the commandments is to love God and to love your neighbor as yourself (Matthew 22:34–40). To embody both parts of this commandment, we pray to God directly but also pray for others. We are encouraged to seek God out in his faithful. We are meant to love one another—any assistance or support we receive from saints or angels or other people is a gift from God. When we remember this, we glorify God and strengthen our relationship to Him. Saint Robert Bellarmine (1542–1621) says, "When we say that nothing should be asked of the saints but their prayer for us, the question is not about the words, but the sense of the words. For as far as the words go, it is lawful to say: 'St. Peter, pity me, save me, open for me the gate of heaven;' also, 'Give me health of body, patience, fortitude', etc., provided that we mean 'save and pity me by praying for me'; 'grant me this or that by thy prayers and merits.'"

Prayers Inspired by Angels

Since the time of the early Church, angels have been venerated in various ways, such as giving them honor, invoking their names, and asking for their intercession. Another sign of veneration is including them in a formal prayer. Some of our most familiar and beloved prayers come from the words or actions of angels.

Probably the most famous of them all, the Hail Mary prayer derives from the Archangel Gabriel's greeting to Mary at the Annunciation: "Hail Mary, full of grace, the Lord is with thee!" (Luke 1:28) This prayer is sometimes called the "angelic salutation" and is the basis of other famous prayers, such as the Rosary and the Angelus. We are also familiar with this greeting in Latin: "Ave Maria" is the name of a famous and beloved hymn.

The Angelus

The Angelus is a tribute to a vital element of Mary's role in the Incarnation—her consent, or *fiat*. The prayer quotes her response to the angel Gabriel from Luke's Gospel: "Be it done to me according to thy word" (Luke 1:38). As Pope Francis points out, Mary is saying "yes" to God here. Her trust in God led to the birth of Jesus Christ and the salvation of us all.

Although the Angelus is traditionally said three times daily—at 6 a.m., noon, and 6 p.m.—it can be prayed at any time. In some places, such as Vatican City or parishes in parts of Germany and Ireland, the prayer is accompanied by the ringing of a bell, known as the Angelus bell. During the Easter season, the Angelus is replaced by the Regina Coeli prayer, which may also be sung as a hymn.

Its name comes from its opening words in Latin, "Angelus Domini nuntiavit Mariæ," which means "the Angel of the Lord declared unto Mary." This prayer began around in the twelfth century as a recitation of three Hail Marys following an evening bell and evolved into its present form (with morning and midday recitations) by the sixteenth century.

The Angelus Prayer

V. The Angel of the Lord declared unto Mary.
R. And she conceived of the Holy Spirit.
Hail Mary, full of grace,
The Lord is with Thee;
Blessed art thou among women,
And blessed is the fruit of thy womb, Jesus.
Holy Mary, Mother of God,
Pray for us sinners,
Now and at the hour of our death. Amen
V. Behold the handmaid of the Lord.
R. Be it done unto me according to thy word.
Hail Mary, etc.
V. And the Word was made Flesh.
R. And dwelt among us.
Hail Mary, etc.
V. Pray for us, O holy Mother of God.
R. That we may be made worthy of the promises of Christ.
LET US PRAY
Pour forth, we beseech Thee, O Lord, Thy grace into our hearts, that we to whom the Incarnation of Christ Thy Son was made known by the message of an angel, may by His Passion and Cross be brought to the glory of His Resurrection. Through the same Christ Our Lord. Amen.

Prayer to Saint Michael

Pope Leo XIII composed *The Prayer to Saint Michael* on October 13, 1884. The Pope was celebrating Mass with a small group of Cardinals and staff in the private Vatican chapel when he passed before the altar and froze. His eyes widened in terror, and he stood motionless for a number of minutes. Fearing he was going to die, his physician rushed over to him. They were unable to find a pulse, but suddenly the Pope recovered and said, "Oh! What terrifying words I have heard!" He immediately went to his office and composed the following prayer to the Archangel Michael:

> Saint Michael Archangel, defend us in battle,
> be our protection against the wickedness and snares of the devil;
> may God rebuke him, we humbly pray; and do thou,
> O Prince of the heavenly host, by the power of God,
> cast into hell Satan and all the evil spirits who prowl through the world
> seeking the ruin of souls. Amen.

After some time had passed, Pope Leo XIII explained the vision he experienced: He heard the voice of the devil boasting to God that he could destroy the Church if only he had more time and power over those he tempted. He asked for 75 years, then 100. God granted the devil's request. The

Pope said he then saw "legions of demons" attacking the Church. The demons almost succeeded in destroying the Church, but Saint Michael intervened and defended her. However, Michael's intervention only came after the faithful had increased the number of prayers to the Archangel. The Pope was so concerned about the devil's efforts that he authored this prayer to help protect the Church. He then declared that it should be said after every Low Mass around the world for 100 years.

In 1886, the Prayer to Saint Michael was added to what are known as the Leonine Prayers. Pope Leo XIII had directed the Leonine Prayers be prayed after Low Mass in 1884. The Prayer to Saint Michael was preceded with three Hail Marys and the Salve Regina (Hail Holy Queen). The recitation of these prayers after Mass was discontinued by most parishes in 1970 after Vatican II (1962-65), which replaced traditional Latin Mass.

On October 3, 1984, Pope John Paul II issued an indult whereby Mass could be celebrated the 1962 edition of the Roman Missal. Due to this indult, Saint Michael's prayer is now recited after Mass whenever traditional Latin Mass is offered. The Pope then asked that all Catholics pray this prayer every day. While he did not require it to be prayed after Mass, he encouraged Catholics to pray together to overcome the evil in the world.

In his Angelus message given in Saint Peter's Square on April 24, 1994, Pope John Paul II says, "May prayer strengthen us for the spiritual battle of which we are told in the Letter to the Ephesians: 'Draw strength from the Lord and from His mighty power' (Ephesians 6:10). It is the same battle to which the Book of Revelation refers, recalling before our eyes the image of Saint Michael the Archangel (cf. Revelation 12:7). Pope Leo XIII certainly had a very vivid vision of this scene when, at the end of the last century, he introduced a special prayer to Saint Michael throughout the Church. Even if this prayer is no longer recited at the end of every Mass, I ask everyone to remember it and to recite it to obtain help in the battle against forces of darkness and against the spirit of this world."

On September 29, 2018, Pope Francis asked Catholics all over the world to pray the Rosary every day during the month of October, concluding it with the prayer "Sub tuum praesidium" (the oldest known prayer to the Virgin Mary) and the Prayer to Saint Michael. In this address, he asks the faithful "to pray that the Holy Mother of God place the Church beneath her protective mantle: to preserve her from the attacks by the devil, the great accuser, and at the same time to make her more aware of the faults, the errors and the abuses committed in the present and in the past, and committed to combating without any hesitation, so that evil may not prevail."

Chaplets

There are a wide variety of devotional practices to the Archangels. One popular devotional practice for those who find praying to angels meaningful is the use of a chaplet. A chaplet is similar to the rosary; it is simply a string of beads to guide one in saying a string of prayers.

The Chaplet of Saint Michael is likely the best-known, but chaplets can also be found for Saint Gabriel and Saint Raphael. The Chaplet of Saint Michael is also known as the Rosary of the Angels. In 1751, Michael appeared to Antonia d'Astonaco, a Portuguese nun. Michael told her that he would like to be honored, and God glorified, by the praying of nine salutations to the nine choirs of angels. He promised that whoever practiced this devotion would have an escort of nine angels chosen from each of the nine choirs as he or she approached Holy Communion. Reciting the chaplet daily provides the continual assistance of Saint Michael and all the holy angels during life and deliverance from purgatory after death. Pope Pius IX approved this private revelation in 1851.

The Chaplet of Saint Michael the Archangel

V. O God, come to my assistance.

R. O Lord, make haste to help me.

Glory be to the Father, etc.

1. By the intercession of St. Michael and the celestial Choir of Seraphim,

may the Lord make us worthy to burn with the fire of perfect charity. Amen.

1 Our Father, 3 Hail Marys

2. By the intercession of St. Michael and the celestial Choir of Cherubim,

may the Lord vouchsafe to grant us grace to leave the ways of wickedness

to run in the paths of Christian perfection. Amen.

1 Our Father, 3 Hail Marys

3. By the intercession of St. Michael and the celestial Choir of Thrones,

may the Lord infuse into our hearts a true and sincere spirit of humility. Amen.

1 Our Father, 3 Hail Marys

4. By the intercession of St. Michael and the celestial Choir of Dominions,

may the Lord give us grace to govern our senses and subdue our unruly passions. Amen.

1 Our Father, 3 Hail Marys

5. By the intercession of St. Michael and the celestial Choir of Powers,

may the Lord vouchsafe to protect our souls against the snares and temptations of the devil. Amen.

1 Our Father, 3 Hail Marys

6. By the intercession of St. Michael and the celestial Choir of Virtues,

may the Lord preserve us from evil and suffer us not to fall into temptation. Amen.

1 Our Father, 3 Hail Marys

7. By the intercession of St. Michael and the celestial Choir of Principalities,

may God fill our souls with a true spirit of obedience.

1 Our Father, 3 Hail Marys

8. By the intercession of St. Michael and the celestial Choir of Archangels,

may the Lord give us perseverance in faith and in all good works, in order that we gain the glory of Paradise. Amen.

1 Our Father, 3 Hail Marys

9. By the intercession of St. Michael and the celestial Choir of Angels,

may the Lord grant us to be protected by them in this mortal life and conducted hereafter to eternal glory. Amen.

1 Our Father, 3 Hail Marys

1 Our Father In honor of St. Michael.
1 Our Father In honor of St. Gabriel.
1 Our Father In honor of St. Raphael.
1 Our Father In honor of our Guardian Angel.

O glorious Prince St. Michael, chief and commander of the heavenly hosts, guardian of souls, vanquisher of rebel spirits, servant in the house of the Divine King, and our admirable conductor, thou who dost shine with excellence and superhuman virtue, vouchsafe to deliver us from all evil, who turn to thee with confidence, and enable us by thy gracious protection to serve God more and more faithfully every day.

V. Pray for us, O glorious St. Michael, Prince of the Church of Jesus Christ

R. That we may be made worthy of His promises.

Almighty and Everlasting God, who by a prodigy of goodness and a merciful desire for the salvation of all men, hast appointed the most glorious Archangel, St. Michael, Prince of Thy Church, make us worthy, we beseech Thee, to be delivered from all our enemies that none of them may harass us at the hour of death, but that we may be conducted by him into the august presence of Thy Divine Majesty. This we beg through the merits of Jesus Christ, our Lord. Amen.

Feast of the Archangels

The Church celebrates the role played by the holy angels in the events of salvation and commemorates them on two different feast days: September 29 is the Feast of the Archangels Michael, Gabriel, and Raphael, and October 2 is the Feast of the Guardian Angels. The Feast of the Archangels is a day for Catholics to venerate the spiritual beings God employs to spread his message of salvation.

While today these three Archangels share a feast day, they used to have separate feasts. Michael was celebrated on

September 29, Gabriel on March 24, and Raphael on October 24. The feasts were combined in 1969.

Michealmas

The feast of Saint Michael originated in the sixth century. In English, it is known as "Michaelmas," a shortened form of "Michael's Mass." It originated as a celebration of the dedication of a major church in Rome to him in AD 610 by Pope Boniface IV. The Byzantine Rite celebrates Michael on November 8.

Michael also had a second feast day, which is still observed in the Extraordinary Form, to celebrate his apparition in Italy's Monte Gargano. On May 8, AD 663, the Lombards of Sipontum attributed their victory over the Greek Neapolitans to Michael's intercession and commemorated a church and special feast in honor of him. The feast spread to the entire Latin Church, and while it initially commemorated the victory in war, it came to be known as the Feast of the Apparition of Saint Michael from the time of Pope Pius V. In 1960, Pope John XXIII eliminated the May feast day.

In the Middle Ages, Michaelmas was a Holy Day of Obligation. In the Catholic Church, a Holy Day of Obligation is a day when we are expected to attend Mass and refrain from work (as much as one is able). This tradition was abolished in the eighteenth century.

In the United Kingdom, Michealmas is one of the "quarter days", which marks the beginning of legal and university terms. Michealmas is indicative of autumn and is the name of the first term of the academic year at institutions such as Cambridge and Oxford. Various countries also have particular foods to celebrate the day, such as St. Michael's Bannock (*Struan Micheil*) in Scotland.

The Michealmas daisy is one of the only flowers still in bloom at that time of year. A type of aster, it inspired the rhyme: "The Michealmas daisies, among the dead weeds, bloom for Saint Michael's valorous deeds!"

Michealmas is also traditionally the last day for picking blackberries. This comes from a story that when Saint Michael threw Lucifer from heaven, he fell and landed in a thorny blackberry bush. Satan then proceeded to curse the berries, stamp, spit, and urinate on them before burning them with his blistering breath. As one might imagine, this made them rather unfit to eat. A Michaelmas pie is made from the last berries of the season to celebrate the feast day.

Feast of Saint Gabriel

Saint Gabriel has been venerated since the Church began. He shares his feast day on September 29 with the other two, but prior to 1969, his feast was on March 24, the day before the Annunciation, which is still observed wherever the Extraordinary Form of the Roman Rite is offered. In the Byzantine Rite, his feast is July 13. Though it was a general feast day to commemorate all of his apparitions, this day was selected to commemorate his appearance at a monastery at Greece's Mount Athos. There he wrote a hymn to the Virgin Mary on a stone tablet with his finger. The hymn, called the *Axion estin*, is still enjoyed today.

Feast of Saint Raphael

Saint Raphael's feast day in the traditional calendar was October 24, and it is still observed where Saint Raphael is a patron and in those communities that follow the Extraordinary Form of the Roman Rite. Raphael has many cities dedicated to him, such as Cordova, Spain. Pope Innocent X allowed the local celebration of a feast on May 7 to commemorate a series of apparitions during the sixteenth century. Prior to the Cordova feast, various dioceses celebrated a feast for Saint Raphael at various different times. In 1921, Pope Benedict XV extended his feast day on October 24 to the entire church. Saint John of

God received numerous visitations from Raphael. As a result, the Brother Hospitallers of Saint John of God's clinics are still called "Raphael Centers."

Feast of Guardian Angels

The feast day for guardian angels is celebrated on October 2 and has been in place since the seventeenth century. Before Pope Pius X reformed the calendar, many Catholic countries celebrated a feast for the guardian angel of their country. Many cities, provinces, states, and countries have their own guardian angels and accompanying devotional practices.

Saint Basil the Great (AD 330–379) taught that "each and every member of the faithful has a Guardian Angel to protect, guard and guide them through life." Saint Bernard of Clairvaux (AD 1090–1153) was an enthusiastic promoter of devotion to the guardian angels. He believed they were proof that "heaven denies us nothing that assists us."

Chapter 7:
Picturing Archangels

What angels look like has preoccupied saints, scholars, and artists for years. The Catechism of the Catholic Church tells us the answer: angels are "spiritual, non-corporeal beings," so they are invisible. They do not look like anything because they are "unseen." This, of course, presents a challenge to artists, for how does one paint the invisible?

While a painting can inspire and intrigue us, it can only suggest an angel. Because we are limited by our senses, all paintings and depictions of angels are of necessity symbolic. The purpose of these images is not to be literal, but to create a sort of poetry that supersedes our earthly senses and puts us in contact with the spiritual aspects of our being. In this way, considering images of angels helps bring us closer to God, as we are reminded that his power and creation are far beyond anything we could imagine or, at times, even understand.

The Directory on Popular Piety says, "The use of sacred images is of major importance in the whole area of popular piety, since culturally and artistically they assist the faithful in encountering the mysteries of the Christian faith. Indeed, the veneration of sacred images belongs to the very nature of Catholic piety." There are many different traditions of Catholic images, including icons, altarpieces, and other artistic depictions. The Directory reminds us that images of angels for devotion should be mindful of angels' holy status and depict them respectfully.

The oldest known painting of an angel is a fresco of the Annunciation from the second century, found in the cemetery of Saint Priscilla. Angels were rarely depicted in artwork before the Roman emperor Constantine (AD 272–337). When they did appear, it was often in human form, without wings, but dressed in sacred clothing. They also were only depicted when historically necessary, such as when an angel was mentioned in the Bible—for instance, at the Annunciation. It is possible that at that time, depicting angels with wings would have been confused with some of the Roman and other pagan representations of winged creatures. Sometimes the idea of an angel was represented with a dove or other bird to indicate a heavenly messenger.

Wings

The earliest known depiction of an angel with wings comes from the fourth century. From that point on, angels in Christian art were generally painted with wings.

In Scripture, there are descriptions of angels that include wings. For instance, the Book of Revelation describes winged beings, who otherwise look like men, as surrounding the throne of God (Revelation 4:6–8). In the Old Testament, Ezekiel's Merkabah vision describes cherubim (Ezekiel 10:6–9) and seraphim (Isaiah 6:2) with wings.

However, there are no mentions of wings in Scripture when Michael, Gabriel, or Raphael appears. What is mentioned, however, is their awe-inspiring presence, as almost every encounter between an angel and a human being is prefaced with "Fear not!"

In art, images of winged creatures are found in many ancient cultures. For example, the *Winged Victory of Samothrace* (or *Nike of Samothrace*) is a famous Hellenistic sculpture from around 200 B.C. Representing the goddess of victory, it has been on display in the Louvre (Paris) since 1884.

Perhaps the most helpful thought regarding why pictures of angels have wings comes from Saint John Chrysostom: "They manifest a nature's sublimity. That is why Gabriel is represented with wings. Not that angels have wings, but that you may know that they leave the heights and the most elevated dwelling to approach human nature. Accordingly, the wings attributed to these powers have no other meaning than to indicate the sublimity of their nature."

The term "sublimity" comes from the Latin *sublimis*, which means "uplifted, high or exalted." It is a bit difficult to define, rather like angels; it is a quality that transcends simple beauty and is deeply moving for the observer, resulting in a state that is perhaps akin to awe or transcendence. When someone acts in a noble and selfless manner, or something "takes your breath away," those are examples of sublimity.

Perhaps angels are painted with wings because the wings are symbolic of their speed and role as messengers. The Catechism of the Catholic Church explains this: "With their whole beings the angels are servants and messengers of God. Because they 'always behold the face of my Father who is in heaven' they are the 'mighty ones who do his word, hearkening to the voice of his word.'"

In ancient times, birds were often used as messengers. We see this also in the Bible, when Noah releases a dove and it returns with an olive branch (Genesis 8:11). Wings are also used as symbols of God's protection and magnificence. For instance, Psalm 91:4 reads, "He will shelter you with his pinions, and under his wings you may take refuge; his faithfulness is a protecting shield." Pinions are another word for feathers, specifically those that allow for flight.

Halos

Another familiar symbol associated with angels is the halo. A halo is also known as a nimbus, *aureole*, or *gloriole*. It is a circle of light surrounding a person's head. Pseudo-Dionysius the Areopagite stated in his *Celestial Hierarchies* that the grace of God illuminates the saints and angels. A halo is representative of the light of divine grace that surrounds a soul in union with God.

Halos have been used artistically to indicate holiness for a long time. The Egyptian pagan god Ra was portrayed with a solar disc behind his head in the thirteenth century B.C. Homer's *Iliad* describes warriors bearing halos. The first Christian iconography depicting halos dates to around the fourth century, in the earliest images of Jesus.

Though a round halo is the most common, they come in a variety of shapes. For instance, a triangular halo is used to represent the Trinity, and Jesus and saints are sometimes depicted with a cruciform halo. The Virgin Mary sometimes wears a halo in the form of twelve stars, which is based upon the Book of Revelation (Revelation 12:1). This symbol was used in the flag of the European Union. Arsène Heitz, the flag's designer, who was a member of the Order of the Miraculous Medal, said that the symbol was his inspiration. He was reading the history of the Virgin Mary's Parisian apparitions in the Rue du Bac, called the Virgin of the Miraculous Medal.

Another form of halo is the *aureole* or *mandorla* (Italian for "almond"), which appears as light surrounding a person's whole body. Our Lady of Guadalupe is often portrayed with this type of halo.

Halos appear to be made of light, which is the most commonly used symbol for spirit. Light is the fastest, most intangible thing we can see. Light traditionally symbolizes knowledge and wisdom; it is where we get the term "enlightenment." Even in cartoons, when someone suddenly understands something, we may see a light bulb go on above his or her head.

Depictions of Archangels

Typically, Michael, Gabriel, and Raphael are illustrated within the context of their biblical stories. These images are often fascinating retellings of these stories, which encourage us to delve more deeply into Scripture.

Archangel Michael

Saint Michael is represented in art more than any other angelic being. He is most frequently depicted throttling the devil, illustrating the passages from Revelation 12:7–9. The visual contrast between these portrayals of Satan as an angel and Michael emphasizes the striking contrast between the two spiritual beings. Satan refused to serve, yet Michael humbly serves and is victorious in every battle. Satan fears our free will because we can choose God. Each time we humbly turn to God, we defeat Satan, just as the Archangel Michael does. His battle reminds us of our own—

and also that we have powerful allies to help us find the way to always choose God.

War in Heaven

The Fall of the Rebel Angels, Pieter Bruegel the Elder, 1562. Oil on panel. 46 in. x 64 in. This painting depicts the Archangel Michael in the center of the frame, with golden armor covering him. An aqua-colored cloak with forest-green lining billows out behind him as he fights with the devil-serpent. He is joined by a multitude of angels fighting alongside him. Behind them we see the heavenly host flying out of heaven to join the battle. All of the angels have trumpets or swords raised in battle.

The scene is completely filled with grotesque monsters, representing the fallen angels that have joined the devil in rebellion against God. The scene, full of writhing figures, gives a sense of active battle. The horrible images of the fallen are strewn with swarms of insects and bloated creatures that appear amphibian in nature, some with beetle wings. Pride caused the fall of the devil; this conflict of good and evil was a recurring theme in Bruegel's work. The fallen angels clearly show the painter's debt to Hieronymus Bosch in the grotesquely imaginative features of the fallen angels. Bosch painted the same subject as part of *The Haywain Triptych* around 1500.

Saint Michael Vanquishing Satan (also called *Saint Michael Trampling the Dragon*), Raphael (the human artist, not the Archangel), 1518. Oil transferred from wood to canvas. 106 in. x 63 in. Raphael was commissioned to create this painting for Pope Leo X. In this painting, there are just two figures: Saint Michael and Satan. Saint Michael is pictured in golden armor with a flowing blue cloak. His wings are golden and blue, echoing the coloring of his garments. His sword is sheathed, and he has one foot on Satan's back. His spear is raised to strike Satan.

Satan is at the bottom of the frame, and though he has claws, horns, and brown wings that look like dried leaves, he otherwise looks human. The lower portion of the painting depicts rock and earth and echoes the brown and rather drab coloring of Satan. Michael is framed by the blue skies of heaven, and his cloak billows around him, indicating flight or an ethereal, non-earthbound status. Michael's face is calm and determined.

Sistine Chapel ceiling, Michelangelo, 1508–1512. Fresco. 133' x 46'. Saint Michael appears in *The Last Judgment* on the Sistine Chapel ceiling. The work depicts the Second Coming of Christ and was commissioned by Pope Paul III. The images in the painting radiate out from the central figure of Christ. Michelangelo had initially painted all of the figures as human nudes, but it was decided works of art housed in sacred places needed to be modest, so a student of Michelangelo's had to paint veils over the figures.

We see the angels and the saints in the Last Judgment together in a group just beneath Christ. Catholic tradition says that Michael is the Archangel who weighs souls in accordance with their actions on earth. He is often depicted with scales for this purpose. Michelangelo depicted the Archangel Michael on the ceiling of the Sistine Chapel judging, but here he is holding a small book that contains the names of the blessed. Next to him is another angel, who holds a much larger book, which contains the names of the condemned. There are also numerous angels blowing trumpets, signaling Judgment Day. In some depictions, Michael is shown blowing the trumpet of God.

A curious aspect to this painting is that none of the angels has wings. While they are pictured in clouds, appear to be moving without support in the sky, and are seen with angelic trappings such as trumpets, they otherwise appear as humans. There is no agreement as to why Michelangelo chose to depict them without wings. Some scholars suggest that because of the great number of figures in the work, putting wings on all of them would detract from the power of the composition, making it too busy. Also, since it was painted on a ceiling, viewers would necessarily already be looking up at it, making it understood that they were looking at angels.

Archangel Gabriel

Gabriel is typically depicted in Annunciation scenes. Depictions of the Annunciation go back as far as the fourth century. The deep, rich symbolism was familiar to Christians at the time, but it is a visual language with which we today may not be familiar. A dove traditionally represents the Holy Spirit. Often this dove appears above Mary (in accordance with the words of Luke 1:35, "the power of the Most High will overshadow you"). However, in some depictions, the dove appears to be flying at Mary's ear. This is due to some early Christian texts that relate the Immaculate Conception with "listening" to the words of the angel, meaning the Word of God enriches and fertilizes the soul. Ephrem the Syrian wrote in the early fourth century: "Like the Burning Bush on Horeb (Mount Sinai) which carried God in the heart of the flames, so Mary brought Christ into her virginity: through her ear, the Divine Word of the Father entered and dwelt secretly in her womb."

In these scenes, it is common to see Mary reading a book. Some believe this is a reference to Mary's strong belief in God, as the book was believed to be a Psalter, a book of prayers. Some artists portray her as reading the Book of Isaiah, which holds the prophecy of a virgin birth (Isaiah 7:14 says, "Therefore the Lord himself will give you a sign: The virgin will conceive and give birth to a son, and will call him Immanuel"). Of course, there were no books as we understand them at the time of Mary; such depictions are symbols adopted from the artist's world.

We often see Gabriel holding a white lily, or the plant between Gabriel and Mary. The Venerable Bede (AD 673–735) compares Mary to a white lily, saying that the white petals symbolize her purity, and the gold anthers her radiant soul. Lilies have been thought to represent purity since the times of the ancients. By the fourteenth century, it was common to see Gabriel with a lily or to see a vase or pot of lilies in the scene.

Touching stories exist to explain the origin of the flower. Some have said it sprang from the tears of Eve as she was expelled from the Garden of Eden. It was of a yellow color until Mary picked it, which was symbolic of the New Eve restoring the innocence lost by the first Eve. The lily was also believed in the ancient world to possess healing powers, which echoes the idea of Mary curing sins. Lilies are also sometimes known as the "Madonna Lily," representative of the Annunciation.

Another legend tells the story of a conversation between a Jew and a Catholic. The Catholic says that just as this lily will grow and bloom without any interference from man, so the Blessed Mary conceived of the Holy Spirit and brought forth her Son, he who is the Flower of all men. The Jew says, "When I see a lily blossom from this pot, I will believe, but not before." Then a lily springs from the pot, and the Jew exclaims his belief and is baptized. This is sometimes said to be the reason a pot of lilies often appears with Gabriel in Annunciation scenes—because the Jew's questioning echoes Mary's own conversation with Gabriel when he arrives to tell her.

The Annunciation, Fra Angelico, 1437–1446. Fresco. 90 in. x 126 in. This is perhaps the most famous Annunciation scene of all. Mary is seated inside an enclosed porch, and a column separates her visually from Gabriel. She is wearing a cerulean blue cloak and appears to be leaning forward, listening intently to the message Gabriel brings. Gabriel is kneeling as a symbol of respect and is clothed in rose-colored robes. His wings are beautifully rendered in blue, burgundy, and gold. The porch on which the two figures meet is cream and gold, in contrast to the lush green lawn and forest on the left. There are many symbols of Mary's chastity, including a fence and the way in which she is visibly enclosed by the columns of the porch.

Archangel Raphael

Raphael is typically depicted in art engaged in scenes from the Book of Tobit. He is usually pictured with Tobias. Raphael is often pointing, which illustrates that he knows the path and is there to guide them. He is often portrayed with a fish and its healing oil, which can represent the soul and the healing of ailments through the Sacrament of Confession.

Tobias and the Archangel Raphael, Titian, 1542. Oil on canvas. 70 in. x 57 in. This work emphasizes Raphael's role as the patron of healing, travelers, and support. Here, Tobias is depicted as a very young child, which seems unusual as Tobias marries later in the story. Some art historians have said that this painting is not a literal depiction of the scriptural story, but rather a representation of the attributes of the Archangel Raphael. Tobias is depicted as an attribute of Raphael, indicating that the Angel is a protector and guide, especially for the children of God.

The Archangel Raphael Leaving Tobias' Family, Rembrandt van Rijn, 1637. Oil on wood. 27 in. x 20 in. This work illustrates the scene where Raphael returns to heaven. The reactions of Tobias and his family to seeing an angel range from kneeling to surprise to turning away. Even the dog that accompanied Raphael and Tobias on their journey appears awestruck. The painting is rather dark, typical of Rembrandt's style, but Raphael and his return path to heaven are bright with a good deal of white and shimmering light. Raphael's path shines and draws the viewer's eye up toward heaven, compared to the very dark, earthy tones of the house and foreground.

Tobias Receiving His Father's Blessing (also known as *Tobias Saying Good-Bye to His Father*), Adolphe William Bouguereau, 1860. Oil on canvas. 60 in. x 46 in. In this painting, all of the figures are life-sized. This work emphasizes the unseeing elements of the humans, where Tobias has bowed his head and his face is in shadow so we do not even see it. His father's eyes are white due to his blindness, and he stretches his hands out to his son, but does not touch him. Tobias' mother has her hands over her face so we cannot see it. On the left side of the frame, the Archangel Raphael is present, observing the scene with bright blue eyes. He is holding Tobias' hand. Raphael is in white, and the mother on the right is in cream, whereas Tobias is in a golden garment and his father is in burgundy and blue robes. The four people fill the entire frame of the painting; we see the top of a tree, a blue sky with clouds, and the corner of a home in the upper quarter of the frame. Through the expressions and the folds in their garments, we can see angst and struggle. Raphael's garment has clean, straight folds, unlike the twisted garments of the other three. The guidance and safety he offers for the journey ahead is echoed in his relaxed countenance, especially in contrast to the emotional displays of the other figures.

Tobias and the Fish, Pieter Lastman, 1613, 30 in. x 40 in. In this painting, we see the enormous fish that tried to bite Tobias as the Archangel Raphael tells him how to catch it and save the parts he will use later. The dog is also depicted. On the right-hand side, you feel turmoil and action, versus the left side, which features a mirror-like lake and a landscape that is almost monochromatic. The right side, by contrast, has the white of Raphael's garment and the blue and rose colors of Tobias' garment. We can feel the fish struggling as it moves from its peaceful lake onto the land.

Tobias and Sarah in Prayer with the Angel Raphael and the Demon, Jan Steen, 1660. Oil on canvas. 32 in. x 48 in. In this scene, we see Tobias and Sarah in prayer in their marriage chamber, while Raphael binds the demon Asmodeus. This painting was cut in half and was the subject of a dispute regarding Nazi plundering of art. It was repaired after the dispute was resolved in 2011.

Conclusion:
Messages from the Archangels

During a recent Feast of the Archangels, Pope Francis summed up their roles in our lives: "Michael defends us, Gabriel gives us the good news and Raphael takes us by the hand and walks with us; he helps us with the many things that occur along the journey... They are our companions, at our service and at God's service." The journey we are on together is our journey toward salvation. Angels, at God's behest, accompany us on the path to salvation.

Pope Francis continues, "They are before the Lord to serve him, praise him and also to contemplate the glory of the face of the Lord. Angels are the great contemplatives: they serve and contemplate, but the Lord also sends them forth to accompany us on the path of life." By entrusting ourselves to the Archangels, we become open to allowing God to guide us through life.

Pope Francis emphasizes that we are all called by God: "We share the same vocation as the angels... They are, so to speak, our brothers in vocation." Our shared vocation is to live a life devoted to the service of God. The very names of the Archangels emphasize that all blessings, strength, and healing flow from God.

The Archangel Michael "battles the devil, the nuisance in our life who tries to seduce us with convincing arguments." Pope Francis points out that the devil's words are: "This is mine." The devil tries to convince us to think we do not need God. Yet Michael is a great protector not because he believes *himself* to be strong, but because he knows there is no one who can compare to God. He protects us by his humble example and fierce devotion to God. It is only through God that he achieves victory. Michael fights the devil because God asks him to fight for us "who are on our life journey towards heaven," and he shows us that every battle is won through turning to God. This great warrior's most potent weapon is humility and service to God.

The Archangel Gabriel "is the one who brings the good news, the one who brought the news to Mary, Zachariah and Joseph." He is, therefore, the messenger of the "good news of salvation." He, too, is "with us and helps us along our journey," especially when we get distracted and overwhelmed by all the bad news and we forget the good news, the one of the Gospel." Gabriel's recurring message throughout the Bible is the message of God's saving love. Saying "yes" to God may not be the easiest path in the short term, but the long-term promise, the light at the end of every tunnel, is everlasting life and joy with God.

The Archangel Raphael "walks with us, taking care of us on our journey so we are not tempted to take the wrong path." When our vision becomes clouded, Raphael is a patient teacher who gives us clarity. He shows us the path that leads toward God. When we walk toward God, we are healed through His love.

Pope Francis reminds us that the three Archangels are powerful allies on our journey toward salvation. They help us remember that God's message of love and joy is always available to us—and that he offers us help and eternal life.

Made in the USA
Monee, IL
13 November 2024